BOB PRITCHARD

COMPLEX MARKETING MADE SIMPLE

Milner Books

GW00597237

First published in 1995
in Los Angeles, California
and Sydney, Australia
by Milner Books
"The Pines"
54 Burra Road,
Burra Creek
New South Wales 2620,
Australia
Second Printing 1996
Third Printing 1997

© Copyright Robert Pritchard
PRITCHARD MARKETING INC
701 Santa Monica Boulevard
Santa Monica
California, 90401
United States of America

Typeset & Design: ADG – Los Angeles, U.S.A.
Printed by: Australian Print Group, Australia

National Library of Australia
Cataloging-In-Publication Data.

Pritchard, Bob (Robert Graeme).
Complex Marketing Made Simple.

ISBN 186351 192 X.

1. Marketing. I. Title

658.8

Library of Congress Catalog Card Number: 95-81861

Other Books By The Author:
Marketing Success Stories
Sponsorships Made Simple
Sport and Event Marketing
15 Keys to Business Profits

BOB PRITCHARD MANAGEMENT

United States: Janice Loveland	Australia: Anne-Maree Huxley
Phone: 1-310-451-4748	Ph: 61-2-99572927
Fax: 1-310-451-3403	Fax: 61-2-99225220

Bob Pritchard
COMPLEX MARKETING MADE SIMPLE

Index

1 Overview

"We need to understand the changes that are taking place, technologically, socially and commercially."

Before we can conduct any business or build a business, we need to understand the changes that are taking place, technologically, socially and commercially.

As a community, be that local, national or global, we are undergoing tremendous change. Five years ago, the buzzword was global marketing, the dream of utilizing the same advertisements and promotions across borders and continents.

After some less than spectacular results, it was realized that not only do countries have different cultures, different distribution and different hot buttons, but what works in one part of one country does not necessarily work in a different part of the same country.

Now, most global companies don't regard themselves as global marketers but a union of regional marketing groups.

At the same time, as the century draws to a close, technological change quickens. Some psychological force creates an urge in corporations and governments to make major advances in almost every aspect of life in the few years leading up to the turn of the century, as if to want to begin the world anew.

"It will become increasingly difficult to reach consumers and differentiate your product."

In the late 1800's, we had telephones and planes for the first time and roads finally linked major cities. Excuse me for digressing for a moment, but thinking outside the square has always been one of my obsessions and to me, Alexander Graham Bell was the ultimate outside the square thinker. Imagine spending years perfecting the first telephone and then...who are you going to call?

In the next few years we can also expect dramatic change, however in this period it will be frenetic.

There will be a continued proliferation of media, communication and advertising vehicles. It will become increasingly difficult to reach consumers and it will be even more difficult to differentiate your product than it is today.

How we sell product in the future depends on what our future is. W: robots make our toast and mow the lawn while we work 15 hours a day, will we only work 4 hours a day from our home office? I think it unlikel People will probably still shop at the mall... because we like it...will st work from our office...because we want to get out of the house, meet pe ple at the water cooler and have our staff more accountable.

I mention that we like going to malls. Well, if we like going to tl majority of malls where currently the entertainment is a pretty ordina fountain and today's youth, we will love going to the malls of tomo row..... literally tomorrow! Malls will be like theme parks, the central focu being the entertainment center, with retail outlets as add-ons. Malls w: be everything from waterparks to high tech centres with virtual realit IMEX theatres, themed robotic restaurants and rides that today are avai able only at Universal Studios. It will be a pleasure for the consumer, product differentiation and shelf space nightmare for brands with reta rental at an astonishing premium. Who but the big guys can afford th development that is now upon us?

Unfortunately most of us will probably work our butts off, albeit on part time, and earn really lousy money...except for some who will make m: lions faster than ever. There will be less government, because we want minimize tax so we can just exist (and governments have managed to tota ly screw up), however my suspicion is that this will lead to more soci problems, more crime, more pollution and more environmental disaster We will long for the good old days and forget how lousy they really we for most people.

The first world will be swamped with old people the government w not be able to afford to keep and the third world will lose even more kids tl first world could save but doesn't seem to want to. At least not if it mear having to do without another stealth bomber.

The average person in the first world will continue to eat junk at much faster rate than they eat fruits and vegetables, however, they will l kept alive longer by an ever increasing list of medical marvels.

Technology will also insure that instead of having 50 television channe that can hardly make ends meet we will have 500 that are losing money har over fist. Electronic billboards will be so advanced we can get more messag per unit of time. Billions of pages on the internet will make opticians the ha piest campers on the planet. In short, advertising agencies and marketers w find even more ways to ineffectively and inefficiently miss their target ma ket. The percentage of advertising monies that are wasted will increase 90%. However, advertising agencies are likely to decrease the footb: fields of foyer marble that has caused the accounts departments of adve tising agencies to be the most creative people on the planet.

"The reality is that traditional advertising will no longer work."

"Advertising agencies and marketers will find even more ways to ineffectively and inefficiently miss their target market."

Okay, so it is hard to predict the future, so what do we do? Well, let's begin with a simple observation.

The reality is that traditional advertising no longer works. At Pritchard Marketing an increasing number of people are asking us how to address this problem.

**t used to be that 50%
advertising was wasted,
w 90% is wasted."**

In the past couple of years, some 80% of U.S. Fortune 2000 companies have undergone reengineering. Middle management has been decimated, everyone in a corporation now has a "customer focus." Open Book management is now the modus operandi of the successful corporation. And it's working gangbusters...for now! The comfortable organization charts with everyone in a disciplined little box with defined narrow duties has been scrapped. It is not responsive enough. We now empower people to make decisions, to be proactive with consumers, to address opportunities and solve problems immediately.

Companies are outsourcing more. This provides more creative input and the addressing of challenges from a number of different perspectives. Marketing and promotion consultants are encouraged to be "off the wall." Find ways to differentiate our product is the usual brief. It used to be that 50% of advertising was wasted, the difficulty was finding which half. Now 90% is wasted and you have to be a total idiot not to be able to put your finger on most of that!

Most companies don't know what their customers think, they ignore or underestimate their competitors strengths while over estimating their own, and they do too little research to get their message right.

The combination of delusion and an inaccurate message causes market place failure, management and employee dissatisfaction and an ever depleting bank account. But, we can feel better by blaming the government, interest rates or the recession. In fact, when apportioning blame we can be more creative than the accounting department of an advertising agency. But we never blame ourselves.

**A plethora of self styled
xperts are writing articles.
's either genius or crap...
think it's more often the latter."**

My solution... go back to basics.

Reading marketing magazines today is like reading a VCR manual. A plethora of self styled experts are writing articles not to solve the marketers problems, but to impress their peers, using jargon and strategies that leave everyone bewildered. It's either genius or crap... I think it's more often the latter.

When they buy a VCR, 99% of people want to record a program today, put the tape away, and at some time in the future put it back in and watch the program. A four year old could write that in 50 words so that everyone understands it. But when you buy your VCR, you receive a 150

page manual that only the same four year old can understand. We ha
learned this from government. The ten commandments set out in ten simp
lines, perfect guidelines for a community to live by. The government conve
these ten lines to 10 trillion words and totally screws the whole thing up.

I have read a heap of figures by various experts as to the number
advertising impressions the average person gets pounded with a day. T
numbers seem to vary from 4,000 to 40,000. Either way, it is a hell of a lo

To be more successful, there are only three alternatives;

- Get more customers.
- Increase the number of sales to each customer.
- Increase the profit per sale.

If you look at each of these independently, all of them can
achieved...none of them represents an impossible task.

Can you get twice as many customers, say from 3 per day to 6 per d
sell them two items instead of one and get them to spend twice as muc
With a little extra or smarter work, providing the customer what th
want by involving them in the process, better customer service and mo
referrals, this is within everyone's grasp. Focus on good custome
increase your share of their business, don't compete in the busine
destroying discount wars and your profit margins will skyrocket.

Think about how you can achieve these results, offer incentiv
obtain referrals from current customers, place an effective advertiseme
direct mail to potential clients. Before you can do this, it is necessary
address four elements.

How do we differentiate our product, impact the consumer, motiva
them to buy and do so at realistic cost? In my view, the keys are really simpl

- Know what business you are in.
- Determine your unique selling proposition.
- Think outside the square.
- Sell what people want to buy.
- Build relationships and empathy with every customer.
- Market the benefits.
- Add value.
- Focus on repeat business.
- Choose your advertising and promotion vehicles carefully.

I am constantly amazed by how many people do not know what busine
they are in. They assume that what they are selling is the business they are i

"I am constantly amazed by how many people do not know what they are selling."

In the past, corporations used to spell out their corporate philosophy in half a page, today you have half a minute."

Today in print, the headline is 90% of the sale."

That means a chain of hardware stores is in the hardware business...right? No, wrong! No one, or at least no one who is in their right mind, wakes up in the morning with a desperate urge to buy a hammer! You buy a hammer because your wife threatens you with all sorts of bodily harm if you don't repair the door, or worse still she threatens to get a tradesman and we all know what that costs today! People go to the hardware store because they have a problem they need to solve... hardware stores are in the problem solving business. Hardware stores who advertise that they have experts to help solve any problem will perform much better than one who tells people they sell nails, saws and screws.

This is actually a pretty easy example, it is not always that cut and dried. Often, determining what you are selling can take considerable research. Once you know what it is you are selling, this enables the determination of your unique selling proposition. In the past, corporations used to spell out their corporate philosophy in half a page, today you have half a minute. This positioning is critical to success. I think Domino's did it best. Their research showed that the major concern of people who bought take-out food was that if they ordered at 7pm, they would not be putting up with the blood curdling screams of a hungry family or friends at 9pm. People wanted take out food fast. Their promise of "delivery in 30 minutes or it's free" connected with the public's hot button with a direct hit. They created their unique selling proposition, business boomed, the opposition was blitzed.

They achieved this result not by offering a good pizza, a cheap pizza or even a hot pizza... you just didn't have to wait. Most importantly, they made price a non issue. Domino's became resistant to competitors price attacks.

In the 1980's Federal Express used the slogan 'We own our own planes' to suggest good reliable service, not dependent on others. Ho hum, business responded and the company was on the verge of bankruptcy. Then the perfect U.S.P. "Absolutely, Positively, Overnight" ...The result meteoric success!

Today in print, the headline is 90% of the sale. People are either too busy, or more likely too lazy, to read past the headline unless it scores a direct hit. Every genius who thinks he knows exactly what the consumer wants without actually asking them, creates his own headline and is amazed by the deafening silence of the telephone or the one reply paid card that the post office delivers. Take the following simple example of two headline options;

- How to turn your non smoking into money
- Non smokers save a bundle on health insurance

A little bit of gray matter and a few well spent bucks would have demonstrated that the second headline would out perform the first by

2000%. The difference between 100 calls and 2000 calls. If the margin $100.00 per call, that is $200,000 extra profit. But the genius did save a fe thousand on research. I guess that is important.

Many corporations have multiple images and reputations to marke One may be to the financial markets, one to the consumer, one to emplo ees and another to the media and even government. In each of the mark segments the unique selling proposition may be different, communicate through different vehicles in different ways. Each strategy must be ind pendent, but complementary to others. The various strategies must b independently effective but combine so that the overall result is great than the sum of the parts.

"think outside the square, there are any number of ways to skin a cat."

The product name and price can also play an important role in the sal success of a product as these factors can alter the consumers perception Haagen Daz sounds much better than Bronx Ice Cream and Clinique sk care's French name certainly positions this American made product. A fe years ago we were brought in by Magic Youth Cosmetics to determine wh their wrinkle conditioner was not selling. The solution? Triple the price! Th results? Sales went through the roof!

The third key is to think outside the square, there are any number ways to skin a cat. How often have you wondered how another busines doing the same thing you do, makes fifty times more money? And the gu running it is nowhere near as smart as you are. And you work much harde Boy he has really had some lucky breaks! Well, the solution is usually muc more simple than that. He probably knew his USP and thought outside th square more often, maximizing his performance and minimizing his cor munication and sales costs. Maybe he also didn't think he had all the answe to what the consumer needed. Perhaps he was one of those people wh wasted money on research! Then again maybe he was just lucky.

This brings me to a story that is one of my favorite successes, so plea indulge me. A few years ago, I was one of the purchasers of a professional foc ball team in Sydney, Australia. This team had failed dismally in another ci and was relocated to a city where this code of football was as popular as a scc pion in your jockettes. As is my usual want, we conducted extensive resear in the city, 168 suburbs in all, to determine a host of information to enable strategic marketing plan to be created. The most worrying of all the resear results obtained was the fact that less than 1% of the under 18 demograph knew anything about the team, its players, its colors or the code of footba This was a disaster as this demographic represented the teams future.

We asked an advertising agency to devise a strategy to address th problem and their solution was a $500,000, 3 year, highly targeted med campaign. They estimated that we could gain 30% awareness in 3 years. wasn't interested in waiting 3 years, or spending $500,000, so our creati team analyzed all of the ways we could impact this target market.

After much evaluation we determined the common denominator was music. We would make one of the players a "recording star." We took head shots of all of the players, with no indication of who they were, to all the dances, discos, high schools and malls and held a poll as to who was the sexiest. One player, Warwick Capper was a clear winner.

We approached a song writer to create a song and a video treatment that would highlight Warwick as a "sex symbol" and would allow appropriate footage of him that the kids would relate to, interfaced with footage of him as a footballer. Prior to its media release we distributed the song and video to every dance, hotel and school that played video's or music and scheduled a full calendar of appearances at these venues for Warwick. On release, we already had a groundswell developed and because it was a singing footballer the response was phenomenal. Every program, news, sports, variety and music all played the song and the video. To further capitalize, we put Warwick in shorts that were two sizes too small and white boots instead of black.

Within 8 weeks, over 80% of under 18's in Sydney knew Warwick, the team and the colors, all from the video and the personal appearances. Over 5000 kids per game were coming to the matches. The agency said $500,000, 3 years, 30%. we achieved a profit on every record sold, 8 weeks and 80%. Why, because we thought outside the square.

The Fourth Key to Success is to Understand Our Customer. We can only be successful if we have empathy with our customer. How many marketers or sales people can honestly say they do? How many understand that customer service is being au fait with the clients needs, problems and aspirations. In my experience...almost none.

Unless we show that there are real benefits in the products we are selling, and can justify and quantify their value to help customers in their cost-benefit analysis, we will go out of business. No business will make a profit unless your customer profits from your product. This comes back to the necessity for added value in today's fluid market place.

Throw out your current promotional material and replace it with customer friendly brochures that focus on applications and solutions that will help your customers. Technical jargon is the kiss of death, 90% of clients, unless you are in a technical business, do not understand it. It puts people off!

The next thing you need to throw out are the employees who are not 'people' people, who do not share your goals and attitudes, who do not want to go the extra mile. Finding the right staff is a pain in the butt, but keep looking until you do. Exceptional employees, not just good staff, are essential to your customer relations.

If you are doing business on the basis of price alone, without trust and integrity, you are also likely to fail.

In the 90's, communication dialogue, not monologue."

With dialogue you actually get to hear what people are saying; not just the words they are using but what they actually mean."

To be successful, you have to customize every element of your busine to be consumer or customer friendly. Remember unless you and your cu tomer both make a profit, one will cease to exist. It will probably be you.

We must sell people what they want to buy, packaged in a way the find desirable. How do we find out this information?... we ask people. the 90's, communication is dialogue, not monologue. The tick the bo questionnaires used by a multitude of companies and perfected by hot chains are next to useless. They are relative to our experience and not the standard required for meaningful results. For example, a person wh always eats in a one star restaurant is apt to tick excellent for every que tion in a five star restaurant, because it is appreciably better than wh they are used to. Is this any guide to how that restaurant compares wi other five star restaurants? No. Dialogue provides the opportunity investigate further, determine experiences, attitudes, nuances. With di logue you actually get to hear what people are saying; not just the wor they are using but what they actually mean.

"No value equates to no business."

The fifth key to success is to sell benefits. This is Marketing 101...s benefits, benefits. People do not buy features or attractions, only benefit We all know that, we don't have to be told, I can hear you all cry out. We turn to any display page in the Yellow Pages, turn to almost all newsp per ads, pick up almost any direct mail piece. Guess what, absolutely fu of features. Boy, I can't imagine why they don't work.

"A change in marketing from consumer manipulation to consumer involvement."

The 90's are also about added value, just value doesn't cut it an more. This requires a major change in business philosophy.

The 70's were about sales...80's were service driven...In the 90's i added value. Quite simply, if you give no value it equates to no busine ...value equates to struggling ...value added equates to prosperity.

The market place is much more quality and value conscious and le price conscious than in the past. Another influencing factor is the growin social concerns of the market place. This has to some degree caused a chan in marketing from consumer manipulation to consumer involvement.

The penultimate consideration is repeat business. Everyone tal about how important repeat business is and yet if you have a look at mo company's marketing budgets, there is usually no allocation for repe business and a big fat number for advertising for new customers. This despite the fact that consumer maintenance is much less expensive th procurement, the profit margins are higher and the purchases more fr quent. You work it out, I can't.

"Consumer maintenance is much less expensive than procurement."

The first steps are the realization that you must change today to be su cessful tomorrow, the next step is to communicate your message efficiently ar cost effectively. That's essentially what the rest of this book is about...read or

 **THE SYDNEY SWANS**

How did the Sydney Swans become the first privately-owned football club of any code in Australia?

Bob Pritchard was one of those keen Australian Football fans who saw as much of the Swans as he could. Working for Kerry Packer's PBL as Marketing Manager, he was one of the team of 'whiz-kids' who made World Series Cricket happen. Pritchard spent several months of 1984 in Canada and the United States for PBL and gathered from the National Football League, information on the buying and selling of teams, sponsorships and income. On his return to Australia in September, Pritchard wrote a paper on private ownership of clubs. Pritchard sought out several people he thought might be interested in the adventure. Pritchard coined the name Powerplay for the new group. On July 31, The Victorian Football League took only two hours to sell the Sydney Swans.

Bob Pritchard became the chief executive of Powerplay and directly responsible to the Powerplay board. For Pritchard and his band of well-chosen marketing professionals winning the game may be secondary to the success needed to entertain and satisfy sponsors. Marketing is where the dollar comes from— only with that, can the rest follow.

When the Powerplay team first sat down to do their homework for the 1986 season, the club needed a whole new image. They needed to achieve success as no other VFL club had done in the past. As a hard-nosed marketing expert, Pritchard knew one of the major chores was to estimate the available market. Powerplay sampled 168 suburbs and found the 'huge' support for Australian Football was as small as 2.08 per cent of the population. The survey further revealed that spectators were more likely to come from the North Shore, St. Ives, Lindfield, the Hills Districts, Eastern Suburbs, and some from the Western Suburbs.

Powerplay devised a visually-exciting television campaign describing the ruggedness of the game, but didn't overlook revealing the cut-away guernseys and tight shorts. They identified it as 'us' against all of Melbourne, plus the fierce desire that we 'Show 'Em Sydney'.

In Year One of the detailed Five Year Plan the marketing division wanted to identify the club as 'Sydney', 'Sydney', 'Sydney'. Ground attendances had plummeted dramatically to an average 10137 in 1985. Pritchard, with his first-hand experience of what it took to make one-day cricket exciting and the success achieved with football presentations in the United States determined that Sydney VFL Matches would have a theme day, excitement, and entertainment geared to the needs of the family. Crowds in Melbourne comprised only 14 per cent women, while the interest of children was waning. Powerplay pulled out all the stops to create fun, colour and movement. They succeeded admirably with their half:time spectacles, providing the visual excitement of almost a thousand participants on the ground, plus fireworks, parachutists, cartoon characters, a circus and a jazz band to entertain the spectators at the ground and the television audience.

When asked to give his operation points out of ten for the 1986 season, Pritchard modestly claimed an ' 11 ' . In the minor rounds, only one Melbourne match-day, an MCG double-header, topped the 39 763 crowd attending on 10 August to see Sydney play Hawthorn, the eventual VFL premiers. In May 37 873 had watched Carlton and 33 192 turned out for the Bombers in July. Marketing had achieved a 255 per cent increase of Sydney crowds over the 1985 figures, with the resulting satisfaction of sponsors, supporters, the media and television viewers. The Powerplay team had won their first premiership!

Excerpt from the book The Sydney Swans - The Complete History 1874-1986
Published by Allen & Unwin 1987, Author Kevin Taylor

2 Research

It is much easier to sell to someone if the product to which they are exposed provides the benefits they seek, is presented in the manner they find appealing and is an acceptable price. Only research can determine the aspects of the product the public find appealing. Research also enables public attitudes to be tracked to ensure the continued appeal of the product, its marketing campaign and its ability to attract sales in relation to its competitors.

The marketer needs to communicate in-depth directly with their current and potential audience and actively discuss the subject with a representative cross section of each. "Communicate" and "discuss" are reminders that communication is a dialogue, not a monologue! Effective research requires active discussion of the issues with the public whose support is sought.

Research is the backbone of success. The information facilitates the determination of marketing strategies to appeal to each group.

Marketers' awareness of public opinion often lags behind grass roots feeling. By the time they are aware of a flame, it can be a raging brushfire. Research enables the identification and correction of a problem when it is just a spark.

The following steps can identify the attributes and liabilities of a product and serve as a path to success.

- Research measures the products appeal among every demographic in the community, highlights the attributes that people consider important as well as identifying the negative factors. This information enables enhancement of the positive and the ability to address the negatives in communication to each target group. For example, research carried out by the Paul Taylor Dance Co. in New York enabled the categorization of their potential audience into two primary interest groups, ballet and modern dance. As a consequence, one campaign features the narrative and romantic elements, the other emphasizes the innovative aspects of the companies repertoire. This effectively doubles the reach of the marketing strategy while maintaining one simple message to each segment of the target audience.

- Research allows the categorization of potential consumers into age, sex, family structure, education, geographic, income, lifestyle and media habits. This information facilitates the determination of marketing strategies to appeal to each group.

"Communicate" and "discuss" are reminders that communication is a dialogue, not a monologue!"

"Marketers' awareness of public opinion often lags behind grass roots feeling. By the time they are aware of a flame, it can be a raging brushfire. Research enables the identification and correction of a problem when it is just a spark."

- Research determines the alternative products each demographic regar as the "competition" for their attention. Research further identifies t reason people find these alternatives appealing. This knowledge identifi the necessary adjustments to be made to the presentation, advertising promotion strategy to address the challenges.

- Research can determine the size of the potential market while ongoir research enables a pattern to be established where future trends an purchase patterns can be predicted.

- Research is key to the evaluation of new advertising or promotional ide to ensure that flaws are identified before they are released.

- Research enables evaluation of the comparative appeal of various mark ing alternatives, from changing the logo and projected image to determi ing the most effective advertising or media alternative prior to imp mentation.

- Research determines the target audience's advertising source and wh particular decisions are made. For example, it is no use advertising in t newspaper on Wednesday for a Saturday event if the bulk of the potent audience listens to the radio and makes its decisions on Tuesday.

- Research allows marketers to be aware of the public's current "hot butto enabling effective planning of the marketing strategy. The public's intere fluctuates according to changing situations and a marketer must be at to take advantage of those changes.

- Research reveals when the public is tiring of some aspect of a produc or presentation, and also sounds a warning when initiatives taken competitors expose a weakness within the commissioning organizatic

- Research can measure the relative consumer appeal of a selection c merchandise or promotional or advertising benefits permitting the sele tion of the most effective for use in the marketing campaign.

- Research will establish if it is important to include give-aways, maj prizes and/or incentives as part of the overall marketing plan. It will a determine the type of gifts and incentives that will attract the public.

- Advertising and promotions can often be too complicated for the pub to relate to, or may be portrayed in a manner that does not convey t required message. Research will ascertain if the public interprets t message as it was intended.

- Media advertising is expensive and must be targeted accurately. Resear can be used to determine the product catchment areas and the consum potential in each, enabling cost-effective media campaigns to be institut

"Research sounds a warning when initiatives taken by competitors expose a weakness"

A small investment in research can save a fortune on media by determining the most cost effective means of reaching the target market. There are numerous examples of advertising campaigns that actually limited the sales of products despite millions spent on advertising. If research had first determined the suitability of the advertising message and measured the effectiveness of the campaign as it progressed, the investment may have been more profitable.

Research provides the key to making correct marketing decisions, anticipating and keeping ahead of the opposition and maximizing the effectiveness of expenditures. The initial outlay on research pays for itself many times over and often represents the difference between success and failure.

Research Is Personal and Logical:

Research should be kept simple, logical and be conducted in face-to-face dialogue to determine how the benefits offered are perceived by comparison with those offered by competitors. The benefits sought by the respondents are also ascertained. Providing the respondent believes the researcher is objective and independent, the answers will be frank and informative.

Initial research determines the most effective marketing strategy and ongoing research will continually adjust that strategy to meet changing conditions and attitudes. Research identifies the most important benefits a product has to offer at a specific point in time as perceived by the buying public, rather than by marketers who believe their product or activity is the world's best... even when the absence of the buying public suggests otherwise.

Engaging an advertising agency or a specialist marketing group without conducting research is unlikely to solve the problems of the organization, as the specialist can only work with the information provided. If the information is unresearched, the campaign has an increased likelihood of being ineffective.

The objective of marketing is to turn non-consumers and casual consumers into loyal, returning devotees or supporters. Unless research is available from which to plan, the direction taken will be on a hit-or-miss basis. Marketing deserves better.

The experiences of other products, domestic or international, should not form the basis for a marketing strategy or to compare performance. Conditions throughout the world are so varied that lack of knowledge of the level of professionalism, differing economies, community attitudes and important local information may lead to misleading conclusions.

Marketers in one city or country cannot copy the successful formula of marketers in another city or country and be assured of success. Extensive "Values and Lifestyle" studies have shown conclusively that even neighboring regions can be fundamentally different.

The reality is that what happens elsewhere is irrelevant. Performance can only be addressed by researching the attitudes of the public in each product's primary catchment area, not by comparisons.

Marketers frequently resist the provision of funds to conduct research

"If the information is unresearched, the campaign has an increased likelihood of being ineffective."

"Unless research is available from which to plan, the direction taken will be on a hit-or-miss basis."

with the retort, *"I have been in this industry for X years, I can tell you everything there is to know. I know the problems, I don't have to waste money on research."* The reply, of course, is, *"If you have all of this information, why are you here?"*

It is my belief that if you don't fully understand the problem, you are wasting your time trying to fix it.

"A researcher needs to combine a little Einstein with a lot of Bill Cosby."

Research is a Dialogue

My basic approach to research has proven to be effective and provides simple answers.

Grey Advertising Chairman, Ed Meyer, summed up my view much better than I could when addressing the United States Advertising Research Foundation: *"A researcher needs to combine a little Einstein with a lot of Bill Cosby."*

Important Considerations:

Research can produce accurate results if several important considerations are understood. These are:

- The research method.
- Sample size.
- Nature of the question.
- Relevant and objective questions.
- Obtaining information correctly.
- Accuracy.
- The necessity for research to be ongoing.

The Research Method

Many traditional product research techniques, where the unique selling proposition, pragmatism and price-point are critical factors, are not effective in lifestyle research where the emotional "hot button" needs to be identified. Many marketers rely on questionnaires and brief phone discussions when they should be discussing the person's feelings and motivations and finding solutions. As a result they are not in touch with the consumer. Face to face research, allowing a dialogue to develop where investigative questions can be asked, is in my view the most effective method.

In addition to determining the communities' current perceptions through interviews, research is also understanding the products history, previous positioning and its previous marketing distribution and advertising strategies. Research provides information on current perceptions, strategies and performance, as well as knowledge of competitors' promotion and marketing campaigns and their relative successes.

Sample Size

People often scoff at public opinion polls that interview only 400-2,000 people nationally to obtain a poll result. They are unaware that the science and techniques of polling are now so sophisticated that small sample sizes will return extremely accurate results. The essential element is the necessity for the respondents' geographic and socio-economic distribution to reflect that of the community. Sufficient people must be interviewed to obtain a representative cross section of views in each demographic. Any errors in this original information may cause an entire marketing campaign to be flawed. For ongoing research intended to identify trends, it is essential the sample size, composition and wording of the questions remain constant in order to achieve comparable information.

In research, it is important to measure attitudes of specific demographic groups. Consumer loss may not be uniform across all demographics but may be attributed to one group.

The Nature of the Question

The questions must be phrased as to not lead the respondent to a particular answer or embarrass them into withholding the truth. For example:

Question   Statistics show boxing to be the most dangerous sport. Do you agree?

Alternative   Which do you think is the most dangerous sport?

A higher percentage of people will agree that boxing is the most dangerous sport with the initial question than with the alternative. The question leads the respondent and makes it easy for them to agree without thinking.

Question   Have you watched the Olympic Games on television this week?

Alternative   Do you intend to watch the Olympic Games on television this week?

A percentage of people will answer yes to the initial question in order not to appear unpatriotic or disinterested. The alternative does not generate that reaction. In addition, people who have watched the Olympics already will volunteer the fact in further discussion, providing a more accurate result.

Keeping Communication Down to Earth

The language used when communicating the message should be in common usage and not the language of the product and its devotees. Many products have in-words unfamiliar to the general public, creating a

"Any errors in this original information may cause an entire marketing campaign to be flawed."

barrier to support. Research will determine whether the communicated message is being understood correctly.

Questions Must Be Relevant and Objective

The questions asked must be simple, precise and appropriate for the purpose of the survey. Too frequently questions do not directly and specifically address the particular issue.

Each market research project should have a small number of specifically defined objectives to ensure the questions are relevant and will provide the answer sought.

Research is not inexpensive and the results, whether palatable or not, should be accepted and solutions sought.

A Simple Example...

If the object of the research is to determine `why sales have fallen,' the questions asked must address that specific issue.

If the marketer has a strong data base, this becomes a relatively simple exercise. Consumers may be asked;

1. How many units of product did you buy last month?
2. How many units of product did you buy this month?

If they bought less units, they are asked why. After their initial answer, more probing questions determine answers to various aspects of the product, their environment and other affecting factors.

A well constructed probe may determine, for example, that sales fell because the weather was unfavorable, people were affected by a major factory closedown, some stores did not have stock of the product and so on.

By Contrast, a Frequent Approach...

Many marketers pre-suppose why sales have fallen and often use the research questions as support. Their first question might be;

1. Do you agree the recent price increases affected sales?
2. Do you like the new packaging recently introduced?

Because the majority of people may initially object to price increases and dislike packaging changes, the first question leads the respondent to a `yes' answer and the second question will likely attract a majority `no' answer. This research may conclude that sales have fallen because of the price rise and consumers dislike for the new packaging.

"Research is not inexpensive and the results, whether palatable or not, should be accepted and solutions sought."

"Research must be determined and analyzed by someone outside the influence of the marketer in order to be accurate, relevant and objective."

This could lead to totally incorrect determinations as to why sales fell. The resulting actions to address the `problem' could include a price reduction back to the previous level, resulting in an unnecessary reduction in profit margins.

Research methodology, questions and data, must be determined and analyzed by someone outside the influence of the marketer in order to be accurate, relevant and objective.

Obtaining Information Correctly

The most effective method of determining the public's attitudes is simply to ask and to do it in such a way as to not influence the answer. Discussion of a viewpoint will glean more useful information than time efficient Yes/No answers and will ultimately produce a better premise from which to determine policy or marketing decisions. When analyzing or comparing data it is essential the information is accurate and all pertinent factors are taken into account. A small error in the research conclusions will be magnified many times in a marketing campaign.

The Importance of Accuracy

If the data being analyzed is slightly inaccurate, the results of the research will probably be incorrect. Never assume information is correct, always check a recognized reference text or obtain the original data. If comparing the results of two or more sets of data, ensure the information being compared is specifically related, obtained under similar conditions with acceptable sample sizes and questions. Each specific market must be researched as comparisons with other markets are rarely valid.

"There has never been a correlation established between recall and sales."

The Necessity For Research to be Ongoing

Research should be ongoing in order to detect changes in community needs, attitudes, tastes, environment and communication vehicles well in advance. It is also a valuable method of assessing the ongoing effectiveness of the marketing campaign.

The success of advertisements and other communication is frequently measured by recall value, however, this provides only a guide. There has never been a correlation established between recall and sales. Ongoing research will determine if the advertising and promotion campaign is actually responsible for selling more product, changing product image, or achieving the other potential objectives

Focus Groups:

This market sampling technique is very popular with many marketing companies undertaking focus group studies at some stage of the marketing or advertising campaign development.

"The essential ingredients in marketing and promotion are an open mind and listening to the market."

Focus groups are paid participants sitting in a conference room frankly discussing the product under evaluation. Marketers and administrators watch consumer reactions first hand through a one-way mirror or by low key participation. The same procedure can be followed with advertising and promotional campaigns. The marketer, in conjunction with its advertising agency and/or its public relations agency prepares a series of advertising and promotional concepts to be submitted to a number of focus groups. Participants in the focus groups voice their opinions on TV commercials, print commercials, brochures, posters, jingles, sales and publicity promotions and other material presented.

The moderator ensures that no one person is allowed to dominate the discussion, otherwise the results will be unreliable.

Focus groups are not designed to replace specific market research. It is a means however, by which both the marketer and the researcher can assess consumer attitudes through direct observation, providing the necessary insight commonly absent in pure statistical data. Focus groups will highlight the reasons why promotions that appear logical and soundly based may fail. For example, for one client we had intended introducing a money and time saving service to deliver group ticket purchases to corporations rather than the social secretary having to come to the sports team office to collect them. The focus group showed that the secretaries liked promoting the event in order to take time off work and come to the sports headquarters which was regarded as "exciting". Introduction of this "logical" service would have resulted in reduced sales.

The essential ingredients in marketing and promotion are an open mind and listening to the market. For example, "watching the event" is frequently not one of the three major motives for peoples attendance at major spectator activities. To a person that is very close to his or her event, as in the case of many administrators, this fact is unacceptable and thus the thrust of their marketing and promotion campaign can be impaired.

"A small error in the research conclusions will be magnified many times in a marketing campaign."

A focus group study we recently carried out among spectators of a major international sport addressed the main reasons why they attended the event. The major reasons were "meet with friends," "great night out," "to meet people," "family night out" and "fantastic atmosphere." To "watch the event" was listed as the seventh motivation. Many people commented that they could watch the event on television.

Consequently, in conjunction with the advertising agency and public relations group, we emphasized the fun, entertainment and family aspects of the night out with great success, much to the chagrin of the activities administrators who wanted to highlight the skills and techniques of the sport, an approach that may have failed.

Chapter 3   Advertising

*A*dvertise vb.:   to call public attention by explaining desirable qualities so as to arouse a desire to buy or patronize.

Webster's Dictionary

The marketer does not create popular products, the public does. The most important element in the success of any product is communicating its benefits to the potential consumers. The public become consumers only after they are motivated to buy. Advertising is one of the principal means by which public awareness of a product is generated.

For every entity with an adequate advertising budget there are thousands with limited resources. Often these resources are little more than manpower, a problem compounded by the lack of advertising knowledge. Even in seemingly professional organizations it is common to be told *"I spend 50 hours a week working to increase sales. Without a greatly increased budget, I can't do any more."* In reality, many good intentioned marketers do more damage in fifty hours than would total neglect.

Television and/or a huge budget is not essential to effective marketing, accurate targeting of the correct message is. It is essential to address three issues:

- Sell benefits not features.
- Keep the message simple and emotive.
- Choose the medium carefully.

Benefits....

It is not sufficient to advertise the features or attributes of the product. People do not buy features, they only respond to benefits. One of the biggest obstacles facing many marketers is the lack of understanding of the `product' they are selling. Often they use advertising to promote the elements that have the most personal appeal, frequently related directly to the intricacies of the product. This may not motivate the consumer. The product benefits, pre determined to be sought by the consumer, must be the marketing focus. The editorial by Jack Trout and Al Ries in Advertising Age, June 26, 1989 is apt, *"More money is wasted trying to change the mind of the prospect than any other endeavor in advertising. Once a mind is made up, it's almost impossible to change. What clients have to realize is that the way to get into a human mind is to change yourself."*

> "The marketer does not create popular products, the public does."

> "In reality, many good intentioned marketers do more damage in 50 hours than would total neglect."

"A simple message conveying the USP will succeed while those that are complicated or fail to make a simple potent point will not."

Simple and emotive....

A simple message conveying the USP will succeed while those that are complicated or fail to make a simple potent point will not. The public is bombarded by product advertisements from a seemingly endless range of sources and will not be motivated by a flat, complicated or confused message.

The Headline... the Make or Break Factor

The headline means the difference between success or failure. This applies to any selling message, broadcast, newspaper, flier, poster, brochure or direct mail piece. The headline must grab the prospects attention and offer a big promise or benefit. It needs to tell the target market your unique selling proportion and appeal to their self interest.

Headlines should be positive, people are looking to gain advantage, pleasure or value from their purchases... and headlines must say something meaningful. If they don't explain what the advertisement is about, people will not read on. Remember, people only buy benefits, they do not buy features or advantages.

Excellent motivating words to include in headlines include free, new, words that suggest a dramatic breakthrough, you, announcing, now, price, easy payment terms, how to and why. Never use we or our, always address the individual reader.

How important is the headline? Consider this example,

Headline 1. How to turn your non smoking into money.

Headline 2. Non-smokers save a bundle on health insurance.

"The headline means the difference between success or failure."

The second headline generated 2000% more calls than the first one. If people are motivated to purchase by the advertisement, and that is the reason we advertise, this means the difference between selling 2000 policies or selling 40,000 policies, getting 5,000 people to your concert or 100,000 people attending. That is the power of headline.

How do you determine the right headline? Firstly, identify your USP and then craft a number of appropriate headlines. Then it's a matter of using focus groups or test sample. I've had a lot of people say that this is a lot of work just to determine a headline. They are right... it is! But in the example above, if the average policy is $500.00, a relatively small investment in research, creativity and expertise means the difference between one million dollars and twenty million dollars in new policies.

The Use of Color

Choice of color is important and applies to every aspect of the presentation. Cheskin Masten in the United States and John Miner's Complete Color Reference Manual both emphasize the effectiveness of color use in presentations, publications, packaging and advertising.

Color can mean the difference between success and failure for a presentation or campaign and consequently is one of the most important, and least considered, marketing tools available. Use of the wrong colors can negate an otherwise excellent presentation. Color attracts attention much more effectively than shape, form or content. Color attracts immediately, appeals to the emotions and determines the next step the consumer takes.

"Use of the wrong colors can negate an otherwise excellent presentation."

Colors have so much influence on our decisions that the color red actually increases blood pressure and heart rate while blue decreases them. The right colors in presentations, brochures or packaging can produce a subliminal effect on the consumer.

Spot color greatly enhances readability and results. The additional cost of printing or advertising is more than offset by greatly increased results, up to 75% higher readership and sales.

For example, the following table demonstrates the percentage of people responding to different colors as a measure of trust and stability.

- Blue   41%
- Red   13%
- Green   8%
- Pink   7%
- Black   6%

In any presentation where money is sought it is important to convey to the prospect both trust and the stability of the person or organization seeking the funds. The use of these colors must be balanced with other colors that emphasize the elements or excitement of the proposal being conveyed to the prospect.

Hard colors (red, yellow, orange) pull the image forward, making it appear nearer, larger, more visible and easier to focus on, giving the accompanying message or graphics more impact. Their brightness increases visibility, creates a warming effect and creates an energetic, vital, cheerful mood. However, while hard colors are good for headlines or bold print they are too hard on the eyes to be used for copy. Hard colors also cancel out soft colors, so any combinations of color need to be evaluated.

The use of colored backgrounds can impart different reactions; green or blue induces mental calmness while pale yellow, yellow/orange and yellow/green highlight the printed message. Blue should not be used as a background color, because it reduces comprehension of graphics or copy printed on it, and consequently decreases interest.

Selling With Color

This extract from John Miner's Complete Color Reference Manual provides a guide to using color in display.

Bright Colors:	Recommended for impulse attraction.
Light Colors:	Good impulse attraction, depending on the color.
Dark Colors:	Little attraction value.
Neutrals:	Some neutrals have impulse attraction.
Violet:	Little value from an attraction standpoint.
Blue:	Essentially a background color, passive, little impact.
Blue/Green:	Has more impact than pure blue, turquoise has good impulse value.
Green:	Luminous shades of green have good attraction value especially those having a good proportion of yellow. Other variations are best used for background.
Yellow:	Excellent attention getter but avoid pale yellows and harsh acidic variations.
Orange:	Red/Orange has by far the strongest impulse value. It is almost impossible to ignore. (Preferred to brilliant orange.)
Red:	Excellent attention getter but use reds on the yellow side. Vermilion is particularly recommended and appeals universally. Flame red is also good but avoid blue/type reds. Do not use red for background except in special circumstances.
Pink:	Luminous tones of pink have excellent attraction value but avoid pale pinks. Coral pink is recommended.
White:	Background only.
Off/White:	Not recommended for impulse applications.
Grey:	Background only, not recommended for impulse applications.
Black:	May be useful in special circumstances.
Grey Tints:	Not recommended.

When considering copy, again color is critical. For example, while 80% of people find blue copy more "attractive" than black, the comprehension of blue copy is only 15% of black copy.

The following list provides a guide to the emotions generated by various colors.

Hard colors:	exciting, vital, inviting
Soft colors:	subduing, quiet mood
Bright colors:	suggest spring, fresh, new
Muted colors:	subduing, luxury, sophistication
Light colors:	direct attention outward
Dark colors:	heavy, somber, serious
Neutral colors:	dignity, safety
Violet/Purple:	sensuality, dramatic, influential, rich
Blue:	cool, calm, trustworthy, fresh (can be cold, depressing)
Blue/Green:	cool, fresh, clean
Green:	stability, calm, nurturing (essentially neutral)
Yellow:	friendly, cheerful, inspiring, vitality
Orange:	solidity, warmth, stimulating, assurance, cheerful
Brown:	restful, tranquil, influential, sophisticated
Red:	hot, exciting, daring, passionate (large areas of red are aggressive)
Pink:	warm, happy, gentle
White:	neutral, stark
Off-White:	distinctive, dignified, safe
Gray:	quiet, conservative, stable, reduces emotional response

The use of color is critical element in the sales strategy. It is important to carefully consider the objective of the various elements of the project and choose colors accordingly.

Choose the medium carefully....

Each market offers numerous advertising alternatives and the effectiveness of each will vary considerably. The fragmented audience in Los Angeles with access to 40 television stations, 36 radio stations and several newspapers presents a different advertising challenge than a city with 4 TV stations, 1 newspaper and 6 well-defined radio vehicles.

Remember, advertising does not automatically mean television, radio or major press. It may be flyers, brochures or posters nailed to power poles.

Among the wide variety of advertising alternatives available are:

Television	–	free to air
	–	cable (satellite)
	–	Pay
Radio	–	commercial
	–	community
	–	national

Press	–	metropolitan
	–	regional
	–	magazines
Transit	–	buses: back, sides, internal
	–	trains: internal
	–	taxis: backs, tops
Outdoor	–	bus shelters
	–	billboards
	–	blimps
	–	tickets
Giveaways	–	fixture cards
	–	posters
	–	handbills
	–	brochures
Cinema	–	theatres
	–	drive-ins
Direct Mail	–	various
Electronic	–	internet

Each of these various mediums requires a different approach. For example, broadcast enables a direct appeal to the senses, print allows a tangible message to be retained and outdoor advertising is fleeting and provides limited time to register with the consumer.

"The key to successful advertising is repetition"

The key to successful advertising is repetition, therefore, providing the targeted consumer is exposed to the correct message frequently enough, the medium by which it is conveyed is relatively unimportant.

Develop a Strategic Marketing Plan

Before placing advertising, a strategic marketing plan must be developed. This becomes the cornerstone of the advertising and promotion campaign and determines the vehicles utilized to communicate the message. The essential elements are product, positioning, price, targeting communication vehicles and frequency.

Product

Research identifies the "product" to be marketed to individual demographic segments. Is American football a football game, an afternoon's entertainment, social outing for the family, a game of skill and tactics or is it none of those things? The same item may represent a different product and benefits to various demographics in the community. The elements or positioning that either exist, need to be created, or be overcome to motivate the public to purchase must be accurately identified. A negative perception can be cancerous and have a devastating effect on sales. It is essential that any real or perceived negatives of the product are understood. Frequently it is more advantageous to address negative elements positively rather than ignore, compensate or live with them. Often they can be overcome by simply addressing the issue openly.

As I mentioned in the overview, many people do not know what product they are selling. This is difficult for many people to understand. Mark McCormack, in his book *"What They Don't Teach You At Harvard Business School,"* provides the following excellent example:

"Many people do not know what product they are selling."

> Many years ago, I was having dinner with Andre Heiniger, the Chairman of Rolex, when a friend of his stopped to say hello. *"How's the watch business?"* the friend asked.
> *"I have no idea,"* Heiniger replied.
> His friend laughed. Here was the head of the world's most prestigious watchmaker saying he didn't know what was going on in his own industry. But Heiniger was deadly serious. *"Rolex is not in the watch business,"* he continued. *"We are in the luxury business."*

Once the product being marketed is accurately determined, it is necessary to position it correctly.

Positioning

Many product campaigns fail because they have been wrongly positioned. To position a product, the point in the market where the best opportunity exists to achieve a market share must be identified. A products positioning is the way it is perceived in the market place in relation to the alternatives.

Every step taken in the marketing and promotion campaign emanates from the positioning of the product. It flows through to all the elements of the marketing mix; pricing, packaging, product, name, distribution, presentation, advertising and promotion. It is simply not enough to have a good idea, a good gimmick or a good product. If the idea works, others will implement a similar program almost immediately and it is too expensive to constantly blitz the airwaves with advertising. Name the company that comes to mind when you think of computers, film, hamburgers, tissues, cola. The majority of people answer Apple, Kodak, McDonalds, Kleenex and Coca-Cola. Why?, because they have positioned themselves better than everyone else. None of these companies invented the product they are known for, but the inventors did not secure their market position. Positioning focuses on the point of difference between the product and its competitors and the packaging of that difference in order to "own" the concept. Those who follow, unless they do it much better, are perceived as an imitator, increasing the difficulty of obtaining market share.

"It is simply not enough to have a good idea, a good gimmick or a good product."

It is not simply the quantum of advertising dollars spent that makes the difference. Each of the companies mentioned above have a competitor that spends a comparable amount on advertising and each represents only a fraction of the total advertising spend in their product category. The difference is better positioning.

Use of Slogans and Jingles As Positioning Tools....

Jingles, slogans and logos can be used to create positioning and convey an image to the market place. Unfortunately, they are seldom used effectively. It is essential the slogan or jingle is readily identifiable with, and relevant to, the overall campaign of the product being promoted. Creating a clever line for the sake of it only confuses the market place. Point of Purchase Media regularly runs surveys on brand recall. In a recent survey on eight advertising slogans with a random sample of 300 women, the highest correct match-up of slogans and product was 14% with the average across all respondents being 6%. While the slogans in themselves may have been clever, they did not trigger brand recall.

Competing For Market Share...

When most people think about purchasing an item, they compare it with the alternatives in terms of benefits and cost. It is important to know the assets and liabilities of your product and competitors product.

Once the strength of the particular product is understood, it must be positioned to occupy that niche. This positioning enhances the marketing potential and decreases the possibility of consumer erosion to other products. Experience shows that those who position themselves appropriately and continue to fine tune their image in relation to community or other changes, maintain their position. Good positioning also makes a product less vulnerable to price competition.

The optimum situation is to create a position not competing for market share. This simply means targeting a different market segment than a competitive product. Once a foothold is established in the target area, various techniques of "fringing" can be used to broaden the appeal and cut into the competitors support.

> **"Positioning enhances the marketing potential and decreases the possibility of consumer erosion."**

Price....

Once the "product" has been determined and is positioned accordingly, it is important to offer it at the right price. Price competition is no incentive to buy against a better product concept and the right positioning. The perception of value for money must be created to achieve success.

Certain short term incentives such as discounts, cash back or rebates can entice people to try a particular product and encourage them to perceive the normal price as value for money. When considering these options it is essential to maintain the price integrity of the product. It is my view that direct competition on a discount price basis will bring disaster because the profitability, and therefore the competitiveness, is undercut and the profit margins are destroyed. People buy benefits, not price discounts.

> **"People buy benefits, not price discounts."**

Communicating the Message....

There are an ever increasing number of alternative communication vehicles available, ranging from television to advertisements in elevators. The combination which will provide the desired reach, impressions and cost effectiveness for the targeted demographics is different for each market and requires careful evaluation.

Different market segments may respond to different "hot buttons" and need to be impacted in different ways. In today's competitive environment, no market segment can be ignored. Historically, marketers have placed little priority on appealing to ethnic minorities, despite their significant population share.

Ethnic Marketing

A crucial element in our marketing strategy is often either overlooked or implemented poorly. Most advertisers in English speaking countries think in English. They design the advertising campaign in English.

"Often, the advertisement created in English translated into languages becomes totally ineffective."

Often, the advertisement created in English is translated into languages to appeal to ethnic market segments and becomes totally ineffective. For example, if the number four appears in an advertisement to the Chinese community, they will immediately reject it because the number four means death. Use of the number eight will get their attention, because it is a lucky number.

The difference between success and failure is research, remembering to address cultural differences in order to obtain the correct information. Always use a specialist from the ethnic community you are appealing to, this will enhance your chance of success many fold.

For example, cognac is a very popular drink among Chinese, so although they may make up a small percentage of the local population, they may consume a high percentage of the cognac purchased in the area. It is therefore logical to utilize a corresponding percentage of the marketing budget in the Chinese community.

Marketing to ethnic groups

Members of ethnic groups respond to companies who demonstrate that they know and care about their customers. If the companies become involved in the community, communicate in their language in a culturally correct manner and the message is delivered by their own medium, the potential for success will be greatly enhanced.

In order to successfully impact and motivate an ethnic group, it is important to;

• Research the market.

- Don't translate from English, ensure it is culturally correct.
- Test your marketing campaign in the ethnic community.
- Treat each market individually, what works in one may not work in another.
- Address new immigrants. They are the loyal customers of the future.
- Involve the ethnic retailer who has a community relationship.
- Involve a qualified ethnic agency.
- Use ethnic media.

The most common mistakes event marketers make is to;

- Assume to know the target market.
- Translate directly from English.
- Forget differences between nationalities, e.g. Chinese and Japanese are both Asian but have vastly different cultures.
- Assume the potential consumer knows the corporations product. It is important to educate as well as promote.

Each element of a community has their own language, culture and traditions. For example, in the U.S., hispanic market there are three groups.

1. Those who read, write and speak Spanish.
2. Second or third generation who speak English.
3. Bilingual.

Using the target market's own language is a sign of respect.

Increasing the message effectiveness....

We obtain messages through either sight, hearing, touch, taste, smell or a combination of these by one of the following ways:

1) Directly. For example, we hear the message and we listen.

2) Extrapolation. We hear a small part of a jingle and the brain recalls the rest of the song. We see a photograph of an athlete and the brain paints an image of the team, sport or event for us.

3) Cross referencing. The brain references the information and for example a picture of a Formula One car may lead the mind to imagine a crash.

The effectiveness of the advertising message can be increased by developing this extrapolation and cross referencing in the consumer's mind, creating an efficiency not otherwise obtainable. This makes it possible to say much less in the available space while encouraging the consumer to create the whole image. This technique ensures that the consumer is more likely to retain the information and act upon it because it has penetrated the subconscious.

By following the simple guidelines below, this extrapolation and cross referencing in advertising can be increased.

1) Initially, all campaign elements are interwoven and tied back to the product by use of a theme that epitomizes the overall strategy. Only mediums which can communicate this overview are utilized in the early campaign.

2) Subsequent advertising of specific elements is designed to trigger the memory of the consumer to recall all the information that is stored, not just the small element in the specific advertising message. This applies particularly to media such as bus backs which provide high frequency but little opportunity to convey a substantial message. If the overview message was well communicated, substantial highly cost effective impact can be achieved, for example, with 15-second television advertisements that might otherwise require 30 seconds.

3) By using hooks to trigger the senses of color, touch, taste, smell, sight and sound. Creating ways to tie these elements into the campaign to enable both extrapolation and cross referencing to occur in the consumer's mind.

Although these techniques are more easily achieved by corporations with sufficient advertising budget to support the campaign on TV and radio, smaller organizations who follow the guidelines and use a little thought, can achieve a similar result through local press, posters and flyers.

Mental Imaging

Research by Statistical Research, Inc. in 1993 presented evidence on how radio advertising extends an advertisers TV creative. The results show that repeated exposure to a television advertisement builds a mental association between the visual and audio elements of the commercial. When listeners hear a radio commercial that uses part or all the television sound, 74% of men and 75% of women created a mental picture of the television advertisement. The study also demonstrated radio's ability to prompt listeners to create images, images that did not appear in television commercials.

Cost effective advertising is the result of correctly researching the alternative mediums to determine not only those that will achieve the required reach and frequency but will enable the maximization of cross referencing and extrapolation techniques.

The on-going campaign....

The campaign must be constantly fine tuned to address changes in circumstance. A products popularity is maintained by constantly improving benefits, providing new purchase incentives and progressively increasing the customer base. This is achieved in several ways:

"To achieve cost effective advertising, maximize cross referencing and extrapolation techniques."

- Enhancing the benefits and attractions offered.
- More accurate and aggressive targeting and conversion.
- Identifying and targeting the weaker areas of support in the community.

All products are constantly trying new initiatives to enhance thei market share. While different products may primarily attract a separat market segment, the competition for support among all market segment is fierce and complacency must never occur. An effective marketing initia tive made by a competitive product must be countered before it has th opportunity to erode support.

"A competitive marketing initiative must be countered before support is eroded."

Summary

Effective advertising is dependent on knowing the correct product t sell, positioning it accurately and creating a campaign that constantly rein forces that positioning. Cost effective advertising is the result of correctl researching the alternative mediums to determine not only those that wil achieve the required reach and frequency but will enable the maximiza tion of cross referencing and extrapolation techniques.

Television Advertising

Purchasing media is expensive and advertising can be either a bot tomless money pit which produces little result, or, it can be cost effectiv and successful. The key is selecting the media combination that generate the most target audience impressions the most cost effectively.

"Advertising can be a bottomless money pit."

While television advertising is not essential for the promotion an development of products, it is the most effective medium to convey th color, action, excitement and emotion. From the marketers perspective television provides measurable exposure and the opportunity to reinforc and extend a marketing campaign.

Ratings, Impacts, Shares. What are they?

Today's marketer is increasingly exposed to advertising jargon. Whil a more complete list is detailed in the Media Terms chapter, an explanatio of some of the more common terms used in television is included below.

Audience Measurement

The total number of people (reach) that watch a particular progran is measured for many reasons. These include evaluation of exposur broadcast justification and estimation of advertisement viewership. It i important to know the audience sizes of alternative program options t enable cost effective advertising.

Ratings

The term "rating" means the size of the audience for a particular time zone expressed as a percentage of the total potential audience. For example, if 9.3 million of the potential 93 million television sets in the United States are tuned to a program, the rating is 10. It is important to note that the program and not the advertising slot is rated and this can distort advertising impression figures.

Impacts/Impressions

The reach (total number of people seeing a commercial) multiplied by the frequency (the number of times they see the commercial) provides the total number of impacts or impressions. Therefore, the interchangeable terms, impacts and impressions, refer to the total number of times a particular commercial is seen.

Target Audience

The target audience is the particular community segment most suited to the specific product/event/program and can be defined in classifications that include age, sex, occupational groups, ethnic origins and income. Program audiences are categorized and the reach and impacts achieved on a particular audience segment can be readily ascertained.

When buying television advertising, it is preferable to define both a primary and secondary target audience group to increase effectiveness and cost efficiency. For example, women 18-24 may be the primary group and women 25-39 the secondary group, having 50% of the importance of the primary group. If station A delivers 10,000 viewers in the primary group and 10,000 in the secondary group, this is an effective 15,000 (10,000 + 5,000 [50% of 10,000] = 15,000.)

Station B may deliver 7,000 viewers in the primary group and 20,000 in the secondary group. This is an effective 17,000 (7,000 + 10,000 [50% of 20,000] = 17,000.) Providing the advertising rate is equal, then station B is the best buy.

Audience Share

This is the percentage of total viewers for a specific time zone. For example: Monday Night Football may have a 10.0 rating and a 40 audience share. This means that of the 93 million television households in the United States, 9.3 million (10%) were tuned in to Monday Night Football. However, if only 23.0 million sets were actually in use, 9.3 million represents an audience share of 40%.

Audience share is not an audience measure. If, for example, 4.6 million homes tuned in to the program and only 11.5 million sets were in use (i.e. half the previous viewing audience), the rating for the program would halve to 5, yet the audience share would remain at 40.

Area of Dominant Influence

This terminology (ADI) is used by the Arbitron rating system to describe a television region. A corporation will define the television region in which the majority of its outlets operate as its area of dominant influence. The Neilsen organization calls the region the Designated Market Area.

How Cost Effective Are Television Commercials?

While television is clearly an effective exposure medium, its cost effectiveness needs careful evaluation.

There are a number of important points which suggest it is necessary to look beyond C.P.M.'s based on program ratings. Television is an increasingly cluttered medium, with the number of 30 second commercials aired across the United States in a prime time week totalling 5,500 in 1993, up from 1,100 in 1978. While clutter is important, recent studies of television viewing habits highlight more cause for concern. Dr. Allen of Oklahoma State University reported that 50% of the time a television set is turned on in America, no one is in the room. Frequent studies have shown that up to 50% of viewers engage in other activities while watching television. In excess of 40% of people do not watch the screen at all when commercials appear.

Also interesting is the Paul Donato research in the U.S. showing that the majority of sport viewers switch between competing events when commercials are aired. When two event programs are aired simultaneously on opposing channels, over half the audience is lost during commercials. In 1992, we carried out a study at The Pritchard Group to provide a guide to viewing habits. Audience response books were completed by 250 households with interesting results. A typical section showed:

	Viewers %
Program	26
1st commercial	9
2nd commercial	4
3rd commercial	4
4th commercial	7
Program return	23

R.D. Percy and Company in New York studied the 1988 Winter Olympics duel between Katarina Witt and Debi Thomas. Advertisers who aired prior to the announcement of the placings rated double those airing immediately after the announcement but still within the program.

It is also advisable to be aware of the content of the program in which the advertisement will be shown. On "48 Hours," a CBS program hosted by Dan Rather, the subject of the program was a critical look at preventing heart attacks and made a pointed and particular emphasis on diet. The

"In excess of 40% of people do not watch the screen at all when commercials appear."

commercial immediately after the diet discussion was for McDonalds and featured hamburgers and french fries. This may not have been McDonald's most effective commercial despite the program's high ratings and the hundreds of thousands of dollars invested on the slot. More careful placement may have been prudent.

These examples highlight four interesting points which warrant consideration.

- Television commercials attract significantly less viewers than the program in which they are placed.

- Viewing audiences are not consistent through a commercial break.

- Advertising breaks within a sports program airing against other event programs may experience considerable audience slippage.

- For every 100 sets in use, up to 85% may not have viewers during commercial breaks and those viewing may be substantially distracted.

The question is not whether television advertising works, it obviously does. The real issue is whether it is as cost effective as it may initially appear. The answer must be no.

Short Commercials

Prior to the mid seventies when 30's took over as the dominant advertisement length, nearly all advertisements were 60 seconds long. In the early 1980's major corporations purchased 30 second units and divided them between two of their brands leading to the creation of 15 second spots.

The average price for 15 second spots is 50-75% of the 30 second cost enabling advertisers to buy more TARP's for the same media investment. Extensive research has shown 15 second advertisements to have 65%-75% of the impact of a 30 second unit and are 90% as effective when evaluated on communication of brand name or single benefit. In event advertising where the advertisement is designed to trigger emotional recall and advise event details, they are equally effective.

When considering television advertising, the following points are relevant:

- The effectiveness of a 15 second commercial is approximately 80-100% of a 30 second unit in terms of awareness, persuasion, recall and attitude shift.

- A 15 second commercial must focus on a simple benefit and stimulate recall of the overall campaign theme.

- The viewer currently discerns no difference between 30 and 15 second commercials.

"For every 100 sets in use, up to 85% may not have viewers during commercial breaks"

"The viewer discerns no difference between 15 and 30 second commercials"

- The cost efficiency of 15 second slots depends on the cost relative to 30 second commercials. As the percentage cost in relation to the 30 second rate increases, the cost efficiency decreases.

Radio Advertising

Radio is an intrusive, personal medium with each station having a tight format and a specific audience profile. In contrast to television programming which changes program style and appeal on almost an hourly basis every day, radio offers regular (usually each day), long duration, specific personality programs. Even through individual program changes, the format of the station generally remains constant. As a result, radio delivers well defined target audiences making it easier to select a mix of stations to reach the audience sought.

Unlike other media forms, radio is a personality medium. People rely on, trust and respect radio personalities, and this trust can readily translate into sales. This is especially true where a favorite announcer communicates the fun and excitement and is seen to give the product a personal endorsement. This announcer involvement is readily extended to promotions, one of the most important tools available to marketers. Radio allows for cost effective, high repetition on-air promotions with little production cost. Radio enjoys many important attributes.

- There are as many radios in the community as there are people.
- Radio is portable and easily travels with the listener.
- Nearly 96% of the population listen to radio in any week.
- People listen to radio for long periods, particularly in motor vehicles.
- People do not switch off, turn over or go and do something during advertisements.
- Radio allows commercials to be immediate and changed or updated at short notice for little cost.

The public quickly forgets the vast majority of information they read, hear or see. Radio has the ability to provide frequency at reasonable cost, the ability to reach a vast number of people very often, to make aware and then refresh the memory again and again and again. Radio has the ability to constantly reinforce the message until such time as the decision is made.

Radio reaches people when they are active, in contrast to television where people generally are relaxing and 'switched off', concentrating on watching a specific program and are probably doing something else during the commercials. With print media people, read stories that are of specific interest to them. Radio listeners are driving or working at the office, exercising, gardening, or at the beach. Radio can entice people to respond immediately.

> **"Radio is a personality medium."**

> **"The public quickly forgets the vast majority of information they read, hear or see."**

The Right Radio Mix.....

In today's fractionalized market, it is generally necessary to purchase advertising time on a number of stations to achieve the reach required. The criteria in determining the correct mix are:

- What stations should be purchased.
- When should the advertisements be aired.
- How much should be spent.

"A different approach on multiple commercials prevents "burn out."

Every station produces attractive figures on audience composition, cumes, quarter hour shares and reach. However, the most important consideration is the selection of stations and individual programs that maximize the target audience reach and frequency the most cost effectively.

The Commercial.....

The commercial itself is critical. It must address in simple terms the benefits of the product, preferably the USP. The opening of the commercial must cut through the clutter to "grab" the listener's attention. If the campaign is ongoing, a snappy, emotive, repetitive and simple jingle is an advantage. This sets the framework for the advertisement, cuts through talk on news radio and provides a bridge for music station listeners. The commercial must be upbeat, positive, emphasize the benefits and call the listener to action.

Radio commercials can be either read live by the announcer or pre-recorded either at the radio station or elsewhere at relatively low cost.

Using Radio Effectively....

To obtain the most benefit from radio commercials, the most effective elements are:

"Humor can either be a great marketing tool or a disaster. "

1. Originality- Sufficient to create interest but not so original as to not appear serious. The advertising must be believable and sell the product benefits.

2. Repetition - A different approach on multiple commercials promoting the same theme prevents "burn out."

3. Saturation - While it is important to obtain maximum repetition, overkill can make the listener tired of the advertisement and this will reflect on its effectiveness.

4. Humor - Humor can either be a great marketing tool or a disaster. Humor should be subtle and part of a series of advertisements so it is not funny the first time and very boring a week into the campaign

5. Music - People have such different tastes in music that a bad choice can irritate and overshadow the message.
6. Testimonials - While word of mouth may be the best advertising, the endorser must be totally credible.

Buying Radio Time....

There are several ways to place advertising on radio:

*   Spot Buy - Purchase specific time slots.
*   Package Buy - 20 x 30 sec spots per week in targeted time zones.
    20 x 30 sec spots per week run of station (schedule).

The number of spots may vary, it may be possible to buy 10, 15, 20 or 30 spots depending on the policy of the station.

An Excellent Medium

Radio's inherent targeting, frequency and immediacy advantages coupled with exciting commercials promoting people benefits, radio personality endorsement, on-air promotions and the ability to reinforce other advertising and promotional efforts make radio an integral part of many marketing campaigns.

Print Advertising

Newspapers are regarded by the public as detailed, information rich, helpful and important in deciding purchases. On the other hand, they are not regarded as entertaining by comparison with television and radio. From an advertising perspective, the immediacy and flexibility of newspapers due to short booking and cancellation deadlines, and their effectiveness when conveying information or price messages are important.

Reaching the Target Audience....

Newspapers have increased in size dramatically in recent years as they have fought to maintain sales. A profusion of travel, leisure, television and other magazine inserts have accompanied an increase in sections covering subjects from sport to computers. While people listen to radio while doing other things and relax in front of the television for hours on end, they are becoming more selective in the sections of the newspapers they have time to read. Newspaper readership also varies considerably from country to country and city to city.

Placing A Newspaper Advertisement

When placing a newspaper advertisement it is important to know the content of the paper on particular days and the daily readership figure. While newspaper readership figures are provided on an average daily

"Newspaper sales figures for specific days can vary substantially from the average."

circulation, in fact sales figures for specific days can vary substantially from the average. If possible, the daily demographics should also be obtained as specific sections on different days influence the sales volume and demographic of the reader.

Three forms of advertising are available in newspapers, classified, display and free standing insert (FSI). Classified advertising is simple typesetting in a column format with a logo or corporate name style frequently used. On the other hand, display advertising is produced by the client in any form and is bought in column inches or centimeters. For example, a 7 col x 4 inch advertisement is 7 columns wide and 4 inches deep. FSI is the insertion of the advertisers own promotional piece in the newspaper.

Display advertising is the form utilized by the majority of products. The major consideration with regard to display advertising is the position of the advertisement in the newspaper. Should it be at the front or at the back, left or right hand page, in which section, on which day of the week? In each market these considerations may alter.

Layout of the Advertisement

The layout of advertisements and the effectiveness of different alternatives have been the subject of a number of studies. Colin Wheildon's research, published by the Ogilvy Center for Research and Development in New York, and *"Ogilvy on Advertising,"* makes the following points:

1. **Typeface**
   Body copy set in a serif face is the most effective and enjoys comprehension five times greater than the same copy set in a sans serif face.

2. **Headlines**
   The headline is read by five times more people than the copy, therefore unless the headline works, the advertisement doesn't. One other simple thing, don't put periods in headlines.

3. **Position of the Headline**
   Readers look at the illustration, caption, headline and copy, in that order. Headlines should therefore be under the illustration and since more people read the caption than the body copy, the caption should include the U.S.P. If there is no illustration, then the headline must be at the top of the advertisement.

4. **Color in Headline**
   Strange as it seems, color in the headline causes comprehension to fall considerably.

5. **Positioning in the Advertisement**
   We read from the top left across the page and down from left to right until we reach the bottom. Our eyes naturally move to the top left hand corner when we open the page. Any layout which forces the reader to change this pattern will decrease readership.

"Unless the headline works, the advertisement doesn't"

"The headline is read by five times more people than the copy"

"93% find capitals more difficult to read than lower case."

6. **Use of Capitals**

Only 7% of readers find capitals in either body copy or headlines easier to read, where 93% find it more difficult.

7. **Promise Benefits**

Advertisements that promise a benefit are more successful than clever or amusing ones. For example, helpful information that addresses a reader's problem increases readership of the advertisement by 75%.

8. **News Benefit**

Advertisements containing "news", such as an announcement or improvement in the product, increase recall by 22%.

9. **Before and After Photographs**

The use of this technique produces excellent results as it grabs the reader's attention.

10. **Quotes**

Quotations increase recall by 28%.

11. **Address the Individual Reader**

Addressing the individual reader in the copy with short sentences using simple words maximizes the results of the advertisement.

12. **Reverse Type**

Over 90% of readers find reversed-out type very difficult to read, leading to poor comprehension.

13. **Bold Type**

Over 70% of readers do not find bold type a benefit in either reading or comprehending a newspaper advertisement.

"Over 90% of readers find reversed-out type very difficult to read."

14. **Column Setting**

Left and right side justified settings are over 200% more effective than when only the left hand side of the column is aligned and 700% more effective than an aligned right hand side.

15. **Background Tinting**

Produces poor results except when the tinting is very light green or blue.

16. **Coupon Placement**

We read from left to right and from top to bottom, therefore coupons should be placed at the bottom right hand corner of the advertisement.

17. **Price**

Where possible, include the price of the product in the advertisement.

18. **Close**

The advertisement must have a close, i.e. why should I purchase, advice that credit cards are accepted and statement of other benefits will greatly enhance effectiveness.

"Coupons should be placed at the bottom right hand corner of the advertisement."

19. **Phone Contact**

The provision of a phone number for further information increases the effectiveness of the advertisement.

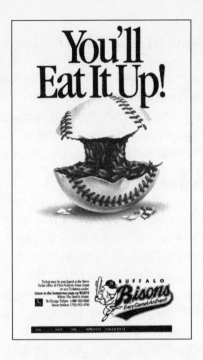 

Two press advertisements from the highly successful Buffalo Bisons awareness campaign.

Magazines and Trade Publications

Magazine advertising can be effective for the marketer. The product can target its devotees through specialist publications with in-depth profiles and specialist information that when used in general advertising is far less effective. Strategic magazine placement can address difficult to reach market segments in their own environment, enhancing the benefit message.

A corporation staging a promotion or a sponsorship can utilize advertisements in trade publications to advise their retailers and/or distributors of the promotion details or their event involvement, position the activity and encourage participation. A sales call to discuss the corporations program can cost up to $250.00 and trade advertising can communicate some of the message at a significantly lower cost. Advertising will not replace a personal call to deliver P.O.P. or other collateral material supporting the involvement but it will certainly provide the introduction. The marketer can extend their involvement through consumer publications with coupons, sweepstakes and event information. This event/product tie positions the sponsor and its product and provides a point of purchase motivation for the consumer. The techniques required to create effective magazine or trade publication advertisements are identical to those used in all print applications.

Conclusion

Although print advertising is expensive, cluttered and therefore difficult to make an advertisement stand out, the respect newspapers enjoy as an information medium can be used by products to advantage. Magazines and trade publications enable cost effective, highly accurate targeting of the product. Careful vehicle selection, advertisement planning and observance of established rules will greatly increase readership and cost effectiveness.

"Print advertising is expensive, cluttered and therefore difficult to make an advertisement stand out"

Non Media Alternatives

There are many effective advertising vehicles in addition to television, radio and print. In these times it appears almost every surface on the planet contains advertising messages, priced relative to their commercial appeal. The key to the effectiveness of these alternatives is their ability to impact on the target audience and to provide the frequency required for reinforcement.

Outdoor

Outdoor advertising is extremely effective, particularly in high traffic areas where their visibility provides frequency with a powerful impact. The large billboards, because of their size, provide an advertiser with "importance."

For maximum effect, the poster should be simple, use strong colors and dramatically convey the message. The largest possible type should be used with the product name being highly visible at long distances.

Over recent years billboards have added moving parts, graphics that extend beyond the billboard and a number of other innovations. Computer generated images have added a high level of reproduction quality, the flexibility to mix mediums and reduced production time. This encourages more creative and illustrative billboards and the use of the medium by many companies previously concerned that the final graphic would not be realistic.

The next decade will see billboards replaced by hi-tech T.V. quality units receiving signals by cable, telephone or satellite. This fiber optic technology will enable advertisements to constantly change and update by the hour or even by the minute. For event entities this will allow information updates, specific event promotions and so on.

The current obstacle is cost, however like everything else, in time it will come down to an affordable rate.

Brochures Or Flyers

Promotion in offices and factories is an excellent method of spreading the word on the benefits offered by a product or activity. Brochures, flyers, posters and sampling provide information on benefits, promote special group discounts, merchandise and seek the sale. Four color material is over 100% more effective than two color and the cost effectiveness of the two options should be evaluated.

Transit

Advertising on and in taxis, buses, trains, trams and ferries provides high reach and frequency. In my experience, advertising on the outside of buses and taxis is highly effective providing the advertising campaign has been planned to enable simple, few word messages to generate impact. With these vehicles on the road constantly and changing routes the effectiveness

> "Today it appears every surface on the planet contains advertising messages."

> "Four color mechanicals are over 100% more effective than two color."

can be substantial. By contrast, advertising inside vehicles, in bus shelters, on railway platforms and similar applications can effectively utilize long copy. After being attracted by a benefit headline and a photograph or graphic, the viewer generally has time to read the copy with undivided attention.

Blimps, Aerial

Most advertising mediums that are out of the ordinary will attract attention. Blimps that display a lighted message in the evening and light planes trailing advertising signs along the coastal beaches on hot days have high impact. However, due to space limitations, the key is tying the message into the campaign to ensure immediate recognition and recall of previously established benefits.

The New Alternatives

The development of new advertising forms such as television in classrooms, waiting rooms and in-store is fast growing.

Major U.S. retailers have installed multiple T.V. monitors in their stores to carry specially designed programs and point of purchase advertising. An advertising supported video system has been installed in health clubs featuring programs designed for the health and sport conscious. Similar programs have been created for doctor's surgeries and dental offices. These programs all attract a defined, captive market and the advertising messages can be specifically targeted. Telephone Advertising Corporation of America's advertising supported video kiosks at public phones in high schools and colleges is an excellent medium for reaching the teenage market. The 14 inch screens play silent commercials. In the next few years the medium will be expanded to airports and shopping malls.

Conclusion

The proliferation of advertising vehicles increases the importance of carefully evaluating the demographics, and size of the audience reached and the cost of the various alternatives. The ability of each medium to convey the required message at various stages of the campaign is also a crucial consideration. Only after all of this information is obtained can the most cost effective media mix be determined.

Appointing an Advertising Agency

One of the most important decisions any corporation marketing a product, service or event can make is the selection of an advertising agency. Therefore, it is essential to understand how they operate.

The initial contact with an advertising agency is usually through the account supervisor who is responsible on behalf of the agency for the account. Account executives report to the account supervisor and in general

"Advertising mediums that are out of the ordinary will attract attention."

The Structure of An Advertising Agency

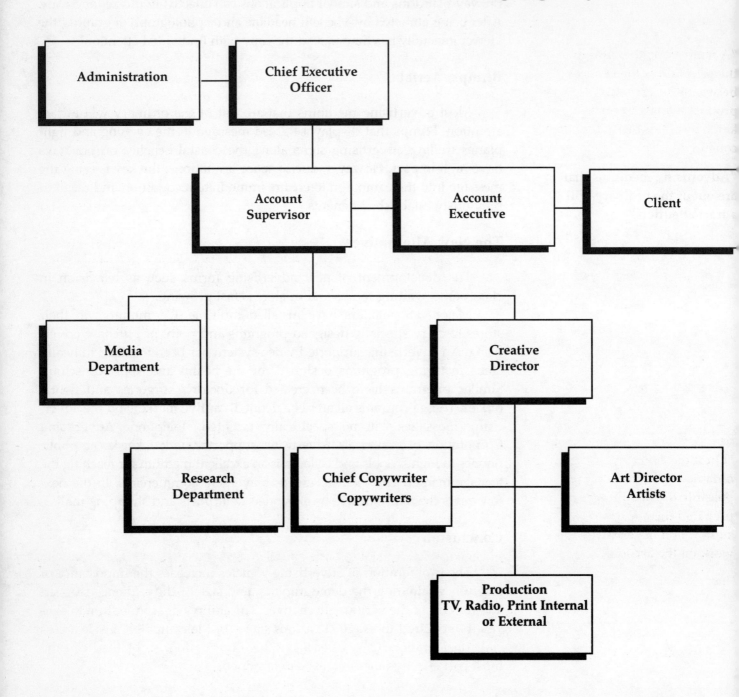

This diagram illustrates in very basic form the administration and communication structure within an advertising agency.

day-to-day business, it is the account executive with whom the client will normally be involved. The account executive and account supervisor must totally understand the marketing strategy required by their client and communicate this to the various departments in the agency.

The account supervisor, in conjunction with the media and creative departments, will determine the most suitable media vehicles to communicate the message. Once done, the creative department through its writers and graphic artists produce the "creative." This includes all graphics, the campaign theme and the copy required for television and radio commercials, print advertising, point of sale material and any other communication forms considered suitable. Once approved by the account supervisor, it is presented to the client, usually by the account executive. The client can either approve or disapprove the campaign, or make changes to it. The campaign then goes back to the advertising agency for completion.

Once the campaign is finally determined, the agency will present the recommended media and the media plan. The media department has sophisticated computerized research capabilities and can determine the media selections and mix that will maximize impact on the required demographics within budget.

The agency will usually engage a production company to produce the television and radio commercials while doing the artwork for print material in-house.

Selecting an Agency

A major consideration in the selection is the synergy between the agency, the product manager or marketer and their marketing consultant. Frequently, the consultant will deal directly with the agency in concert with, or on the product managers behalf.

The selection should never be based solely on any submission the agency may provide as an illustration of their abilities. Many agencies engage freelance talent to write speculative submissions and these may not reflect the capability of the agency. Once the agency has obtained the account, it is possible the people who prepared the approved submission never again work on the account. Also, while the submitted creative may provide a guide, an agency is selected to provide a range of functions not just one creative idea. At this stage the presented campaign is unlikely to have relevance to the actual marketing needs of the client.

In selecting the right agency, the first step is to be totally clear about the type of agency and the services required. Personally, I always look for a small agency that produces highly creative and emotional work and where we have direct personal contact with the principal. It is easy to buy technicians, good creativity is rare.

How Much Will It Cost?

In general, agencies charge a creative fee in addition to a commission up

---

"A major consideration in the selection is the synergy between the agency, the product manager or marketer and their marketing consultant."

"Once the agency has obtained the account, it is possible the people who prepared the approved submission never again work on the account."

"It is easy to buy technicians, good creativity is rare."

"It is essential to maintain a tight control on expenditure to ensure the agency is managing the advertising dollar efficiently."

to 17.5% on media placement, although many advertisers negotiate lower commissions and other arrangements. These may include a flat fee, a fee and reduced commission and an increasing number are performance based. Expenditure on media, promotion and production can rapidly get out of control and therefore the total costs involved in every aspect of the advertising campaign must be fully detailed. For example, a quotation for a newspaper advertisement space may be $2,000, however artwork and other costs may be a further $2,000. A printer may quote $1,000 to print a particular item but the plates and negatives may be a further $1,000. Always seek the all up cost, including tax and agency service fee, as advertising production can involve justifiable charges that add up very rapidly.

It is essential to maintain a tight control on expenditure to ensure the agency is managing the advertising dollar efficiently.

What are the Criteria?

The considerations that should be made in selecting an agency are:

1.   Define the requirements of the product and the expectations held for the agencies performance.
2.   Prepare a list of three agencies that fit the requirements and obtain a written presentation of their credentials.
3.   The final decision should be based on the following:

- Does the agency have a conflict of interest? This does not simply mean a competitive product, it includes all potential forms of conflict.
- Personality, structure and experience of the principals and management.
- Access to the principals.
- The experience of the people who will actually work on the account.
- The way the account director perceives the product and its requirements.
- The accounts importance to the agency.
- How well you relate to the creative team that will work on the account.
- Their interest and understanding of the clients industry, not necessarily the specific product under consideration.
- Their reliability.
- The standard of their creative, finished art and presentations.
- Their cost of services over and above service fees.

It is advisable to discuss the agency's performance with current clients, preferably accounts of a similar size.

Summary

The combination of an astute marketer, excellent research and an, aggressive, emotional and creative agency is impossible to beat when marketing a product. The most important ingredients are research, tight financial control, creative marketing, a long term plan and a lot of hard work. That combination is infallible.

4 Media and Advertising Terms

Media exposure, either in the form of news coverage, or as advertising and promotion, is critical to the success of a product. To maximize the benefits media offers, it is essential to have a strong working knowledge of the industry.

One of the most confusing aspects of dealing with the media or with advertising agencies is the plethora of unique terminology. It is important to understand these terms in order to communicate in this critical area of the marketing business.

Outlined below are some of the most common terms.

Ad Page Exposure	How many readers look at an average advertising page in a particular publication issue.
AM (Radio)	Amplitude Modulation is a system of radio transmission in which the sound wave is modulated by changing its amplitude (as distinct from FM - frequency modulation).
Arbitron	Use daily method to determine local ratings
Attention	The degree to which the audience pays "attention" to commercial messages.
Audience	The number of people who see a particular program or advertising message.
Audience Composition	Describes the audience breakdown into various classifications.
Audience Flow	The movement in audience from station to station (radio/TV) at a given point in time, i.e. people have several alternatives: turn on, remain listening, change stations or switch off. This is important for programming purposes.
Audience Share	The audience expressed in relation to the percentage of sets actually in use. The other common measurement is "ratings" which is the percentage of total potential audience.
Audience Skew	Describes the particular audience type when it does not represent the community average,i.e. "skewed to over-40's".

Audit   Independent assessment of audience level

Average Audience   Estimated average audience of a particula
                              station over a stated period of time.

Average Frequency   The average number of times people or hom
                              are exposed to the schedule of commercials.

$$AF = \frac{\text{Gross Rating Points}}{\text{Net Rating Points}} \quad \frac{\text{(Ttl impacts)}}{\text{(Reach)}}$$

Bias   Also called statistical error. Takes into accoun
                              the bias in the collection of data, e.g. a tele
                              phone survey has a bias against those witho
                              a telephone.

Birch   Use telephone interviews to determine loc
                              ratings.

Bleed   Advertisements that run to the edge of a pag
                              without a margin.

Bromide/Slick   Black and white photographic reproductio
                              of an image. Used for print advertising.

Checkerboarding   Placement of a program in a different time
                              slot each day.

Circulation   Net paid sales of a particular publication.

Classified Advertisement An advertisement placed in a class with simil
                              messages.

Column Inch   (or column centimeter) The measurement
                              print space. One column inch refers to a siz
                              one column wide and one inch deep. Fiv
                              column inches could refer to a space one colum
                              wide and five inches deep or five columr
                              wide and one inch deep.

Color Penetration   Number of people with a color TV set.

Controlled Circulation   People who qualify for a free issue of a magazin

Cost Effectiveness   The cost of using the media per thousan
                              impacts, or cost per target audience ratin
                              point (TARP).

Cost Per Point   Cost per rating point.

Cost Per TARP   The cost of advertising to reach each 1% of th
                              target audience with a particular type of medi

Cost Per Thousand   The cost involved in reaching each 1,000 peop
                              per media vehicle.

Coverage   The geographic coverage of a medium.

Cross Section   A demographically selected section of the surve

Cumulative Audience   Cumes (reach) is the number of different peop
                              (or households) reached at least once by th
                              medium or by a specific number of advertise
                              ments. For example, a bus on a particular rout
                              may carry a total of 100 different passenger
                              (cumes), however the average number of

passengers at any time may be 20 (average audience).

Daily Cumulative	As above, but applicable to one specific day.
Demographics	Audience classifications by age, sex, suburb, income, etc.
Display Advertising	A type and/or graphic composition designed as a feature advertisement.
Duplicated Audience	The number of people exposed to a multiplicity of vehicles in the one media type.
Exclusive Audience	Number of target audience only reached by a specific media vehicle.
Extrapolation	Projecting a result beyond its survey audience.
Frequency Distribution	The number of times an audience has seen a given commercial, i.e.

20% of homes saw commercial once.
20 x 1 = 20
10% of homes saw commercial twice.
10 x 2 = 20
7% of homes saw commercial 3 times.
7 x 3 = 21
3% of homes saw commercial 4 times.
3 x 4 = 12
i.e. 40% of homes saw the commercial once. The advertisement produced a total of 73 Gross Rating Points.

Flighting	Continuity of impression in the absence of actual advertising.
FM Modulation	Transmitted radio wave is modulated in accordance with the amplitude and pitch of the signal.
Gross Rating Points	The total of the ratings of the various media utilized in a schedule. This means the total weight delivered by the schedule without regard to duplication. This is measured as a percentage. Total impacts or impressions is an equivalent measure expressed in thousands.
Homes Using Television	The percentage of homes where at least 1 television set is switched on at any one time. The sum of ratings of all stations can exceed the HUT because of multiple set watching. The term HUT has replaced the old terminology "set in use" - SIU.
Horizontal Publication	Covers one job category within a number of industries.
Impacts	The total number of times that a commercial is seen or heard. The total reach multiplied by the frequency (the number of times it is seen or heard) gives the total number of impacts.

Media Mix   Combination of media vehicles used in a campaign.

Median   Same proportion of sample on either side of the median.

Media Vehicle   Refers to the particular station, newspaper other advertising form.

MSA   Metropolitan Survey Area is the area of concentrated audience for a station.

Rating Points   The size of an audience expressed as a percentage of the total available listeners or viewer Radio ratings are taken in 1/4-hour segment In television, complete programs are rated.

Out-of-home-advertising Updated term for outdoor advertising.

Page Traffic   The proportion of a publication's readers wh look at an individual page in a publication.

Penetration   The total coverage of a particular media vehicl or medium.

Point Size   A unit about 1/72 inch used to measure th dimension of printing type.

Potential   The total number of people in a particular are in a specific demographic.

Profile   The composition of the audience of a partic ular media vehicle.

Psychographic Research Reasons behind a consumers behavior.

"Q" ratings   Measure of popularity rather than audience siz

Qualitative Data   Research to understand behavioral pattern "why" people do things.

Quantitative Data   Research to understand "how many" peopl behave a particular way.

"RADAR"   Radio All-Dimension Audience Research, ne work ratings through telephone interviews.

Random Sample   Selection of research subjects at random.

Ratings   The size of an audience expressed as a per centage of the total potential.

Reach   The total number of people that see or hea a commercial.

Readership   The total number of people reading a partic ular publication.

Remnant Space   Space created by unbought partial-run ads in other editions of newspapers.

Reverse Type   The technique of printing the background an not the image to be projected. This allows th image to appear although unprinted and i reverse to the norm.

Rotation   Movement of a commercial from one time zon to another in a particular rate zone.

Run of Schedule	(or RUN OF STATION) Scheduling a series of advertisements to attain the maximum potential reach of a particular media vehicle.
Sample	Describes the group surveyed. The sample must be representative of the population from which it is drawn.
Schedule	The appearance times schedule of advertisement.
Share of Audience	The percentage of the total audience at a particular time period tuned to a particular station.
Slick	see BROMIDE
Spot Advertising	National advertisers buying station-by-station rather than through networks.
Socio-Economic	Classifications of people based on income, occupation, suburb, etc.
Stripping	Placement of a program in the same time slot each day.
Target Audience	The most appropriate audience for a particular product defined in a number of terms including age sex, occupational groups, income, etc.
TARP	Target Audience Rating Point (or PRP, People Rating Point) is the percentage of the target audience reached at a particular time with a specific media vehicle.
Total Impacts	The total number of people delivered by an advertising schedule, including duplication.
TVF	The measure of "familiarity" of a particular TV program.
TVQ	The measure of "liking" of a particular TV program.
Type Face	Describes the faces of the printing type and the image projected. Distinguishes type as an identifiable style.
Typeset	To set the words in type.
UHF	Any frequency between 300 and 3,000 megahertz.
Up-front Buys	Commercials bought at a premium at the opening of the buying season.
Vertical Publication	Cover all aspects of a single industry.
VHF	Any frequency between 30 and 300 megacycles per second.
Viewers Per Set	Total audience divided by the number of sets tuned to a particular program.
Weekly Cumulative	The proportion or number of different people reached at least once by a number of particular advertisements in a week.

Zone	A period of time defined by the specific media vehicle
Zone Average	Estimated audience in percentage or number achieved by a specific station during a time zone
Zone Cumulative	Estimated cumulative audience as above.

While this is not an exhaustive list, it includes the most frequently used terms to enable comprehension of media and advertising jargon.

Chapter 5   Public Relations

Chapter

Public relations, or PR, is one of the most powerful marketing tools available. With escalating media costs and the often limited resources of many entities, it is essential to maximize the less expensive forms of exposure that are available. Corporations also seek to maximize their exposure by the most cost effective means. Consequently, there is a growing emphasis on non-media marketing, with disciplines such as Public Relations, Promotions, Direct and Incentive Marketing enjoying rapid growth at the expense of traditional advertising.

Public Relations is not simply obtaining 'free publicity' but is part of a carefully planned mix of advertising (above the line) and 'below the line' disciplines mentioned above. Public relations builds an image in terms of credibility and recognition, creating a favorable attitude to the activity or product by means that are not seen to be 'hard sell'. Advertising is self-praise and is expected to be complimentary, while public relations reflects what others are saying and therefore carries more weight with the public. This form of exposure is far more credible than direct advertising. News stories that are part of a PR campaign generate seven times the response of an advertising campaign.

> News stories that are part of a PR campaign generate seven times the response of an advertising campaign."

Specific Item Recall

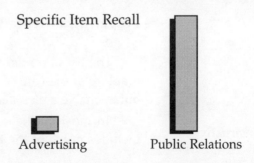

Advertising   Public Relations

In a 15, 30 or 60 second radio or television spot, the focus must be on a single simple point to be effective, while Public Relations allows discussion of the issues, the personnel involved, explains the background or features human interest stories. Put simply, advertising takes a single point and hammers it home, creating short term awareness of one small component. PR on the other hand, communicates a more complex message explained in detail and has a long term effect.

Publicity is not easy to obtain. Raising awareness and obtaining effective public relations and media exposure is not simply a matter of knowing the journalists. There are a wealth of activities and products competing

> Publicity is not easy to obtain. It is not simply a matter of knowing the journalists."

for the little valuable space available on the air or in print. The media i dependent on readership, listening or viewing audience for its success an its obligation is to provide interesting, informative stories, not to suppor any particular product. Therefore, if the information is not interesting, i will not receive coverage. The media owes no favors.

Public Relations has an important role in providing feedback to th product or activity from the media and the public during each of the thre phases in any program; development, implementation and evaluation. Thi information is valuable in determining marketing strategies, planning direc response material, monitoring coverage and awareness, and ascertainin; perceptions and attitudes of the media, public and other concerned parties.

There is an old expression, *"All publicity is good publicity providing the spell your name right."* In my view this is not true, as while bad publicit raises the immediate profile, it is destructive in the long term.

The media can be a vital ingredient in the success of a product and believe it is essential to take journalists into confidence. The more infor mation provided, the better the understanding and the increased likeli hood of informed stories that will assist the entity to achieve its objectives

Journalists are measured on the originality, quality and accuracy o their articles and the public is not interested in old news, so the same stor should not be provided to more than one journalist in any media vehicle Interesting new angles must be initiated. At media conferences, ever opportunity must be provided for journalists to conduct private inter views in order to develop individual storylines.

The essential ingredients of PR are thorough planning, interestin; stories and a good media relationship.

Preparing a Media List

The list of media vehicles and the contacts, audience reach and demo graphics of each are of immense importance, not only for publicity purpose but to enable a message to effectively impact a specific target market.

In most markets, a media listing book is published regularly whicl includes much of the required information. Among these are:

Australia	Margaret Gees Media Guide
U. S. A.	Broadcast Yearbook
	Bacons Publicity Checker
Canada	Matthews Media Listing
United Kingdom	Pims Media Directory

For easy reference, the lists are categorized by media type according to thei specialization, whether national, metropolitan or regional and by city and state

---

"The media is dependent on readership, listening or viewing audience for its success and its obligation is to provide interesting, informative stories, not to support any particular product."

"Bad publicity is destructive in the long term."

Television and Radio

While many publicity items are designed to achieve broad coverage, often the most important ones are those created to impact a particular market segment and achieve a specific goal. It is only through knowledge of all the available exposure alternatives, their format, ratings and audience demographics can the most effective placement be determined. For example, obtaining an interview on the top rating program may provide extensive reach but may be ineffective if the audience being attracted is not the required target audience. A program rating number three or four may deliver more of the target audience than the top rating program. This also applies to advertising, where increased effectiveness and considerable savings can be achieved by specific time slot placement rather than buying on the basis of the stations overall target market rating. In addition to the knowledge of on-air personalities and their producers, it is important to identify freelance journalists who conduct on-location interviews and also the news, financial, business, sports, entertainment, community affairs or promotions directors, whichever is beneficial. It is frequently possible to extend the exposure by creating a specific promotion in association with the station or developing a new angle involving a specialist journalist.

Radio

To be able to readily identify the most appropriate placement of publicity, it is important to consider the stations format. Radio stations have a consistent format throughout the day and the week. While the on-air personality may change, the format remains constant. For this reason radio stations have very defined audiences. The key is to utilize the station that best addresses your target market and the personality(s) that best reflect your image.

Television

By contrast with radio, television programs vary in content and audience demographics on an hour to hour, program to program basis. It is therefore much more difficult to reach your target audience and considerable research must be undertaken on audience demographics for particular programs.

Newspapers and Magazines

In addition to seeking major features, personality profiles and special programs in specific publications, columnists in all print media can be constantly provided with interesting items appropriate to their columns. Where appropriate, items should be included in the children's section in the form of illustrations, color-in or drawing competitions. As is the case with other media, every opportunity should be seized to extend the promotion through editorial or competitions.

"Obtaining an interview on the top rating program may provide extensive reach but may be ineffective if the audience is not the required target audience."

Additions to the Contact List

It is beneficial to include on the media list, contact details for prom nent politicians and officials who may be of some assistance to the orgar zation either now or in the future.

The media release may create an awareness that leads to an otherwi unforeseen opportunity. For example, the particular program may coi cide with a politician's schedule or take place in their constituency, anot er entity may be seeking a promotional opportunity or a local communi group may be looking for a local activity to support.

Planning an Effective P.R. Campaign

For a public relations campaign to be effective, a balanced mix of conti uous exposure must be obtained across all media vehicles. This should includ

- Specialist information for the devotee; benefits, applications, st tistics, participants, nature of the performance, etc.
- Public affinity snippets; personalities, humor and activities mentioned in columns and social pages.
- Personality articles or interviews.
- Sponsor involvement.
- Competitions.
- Imaging items, community, charity.
- Feature stories to increase public identification.
- Personality affinity with the public; common interests; location of residence, type of employment, hobbies.
- Public appearances, speeches, clinics.
- Program update facsimiles.
- Provision of B-Roll footage to news outlets.

To achieve this exposure, every publication, electronic media or anci lary vehicle that impacts the potential audience is determined, the appr priate personality selected and an effective publicity angle created.

The PR Media Plan...

Once the media list is compiled, the alternatives prioritized and th story angle determined, each producer, journalist or editor is contacted ascertain the exposure potential of the item.

The various publicity elements are scheduled according to a critic path to ensure that the interest and exposure is maintained throughout th required period. Special emphasis is placed on specific stories at particul times to reinforce the marketing and promotion strategy.

"Place special emphasis on specific stories timed to coincide with announce-ments, advertising in promotional campaigns,"

Among the vehicles that can be used effectively are:

- Magazines and newspapers
- Radio and television
- Electronic, Internet publishing
- Video news releases
- Travel writers packages
- Ancillary activities such as speeches, public appearances

Magazines and Newspapers...

Information to satisfy the needs of the devotee of the activity should be regularly supplied to the specialist journalist. However, this information is only reaching the tip of the potential audience iceberg. Significantly broader exposure must be obtained.

There is a profusion of print media with substantial and diverse readership which provides a constant source of publicity opportunities for many products and their sponsors. These stories constantly broaden the potential consumer base. The following can be approached:

- In-flight magazines
- Business magazines
- Advertising and Media trade publications
- "This week in........" publications
- Radio and TV publications

Radio and Television...

Public relations can be used to extend television and radio publicity by incorporating:

- Competitions, merchandise or product giveaways
- Personality profiles
- Event education, tips
- Historical events
- Personality interviews
- Appearances on programs

Exposure may be obtained on game shows, children's programs, music video and talk shows, and sports and entertainment programs.

Video News Releases....

The provision of high impact video excerpts of product/project preparation, highlights of previous activities, profiles of participants, etc, provides television broadcasters with air quality supplemental footage for newscasts and stand-alone features to fill time slots.

B-roll....

Gathering footage on the opening of the event, tape interview footage of attendees, shows, etc... can produce valuable exposure. Th footage is rushed to networks who wish to cover the event but, perhar lack the available resources to obtain live footage.

Travel Writers Package....

Information can be provided to tour operators and publishers of trav el and hospitality publications and brochures to encourage visitors t attend an event.

Ancillary Exposure....

It is necessary to plan as many targeted presentations as possible. Thes may consist of a video presentation and speech by a personality to spor clubs, large fraternal/social clubs, community groups or charity organiza tions. Each city has a large number of these groups with substantial men bership and a face-to-face opportunity should be seized whenever possible

Public Service Announcements....

Non-profit associations are eligible for promotion through both tele vision and radio PSA's. For radio, 30 and 60 second formats should b disseminated to all AM and FM radio stations while 30 second televisio advertisements should be sent to the television stations.

Have Empathy With The Media:

Powerplay International Limited

Journalists work under constant deadline pressures and to gain the support and maximize exposure opportunities, it is essential to understan the workings of their industry. The following tips will be of benefit:

Effective Story Placement....

- Identify the journalist most appropriate for the particular story angle and meet with them personally, enabling them to be motivated by your dedication and enthusiasm. In addition, it is frequently advantageous to know the editor and sub-editor at newspapers and magazines, or the program producer in the case of electronic media.
- Take an interest in the journalists' affairs, be a friend and develop empathy.
- Know the deadlines for each publication, radio and television program. Journalists, producers and editors work to tight deadlines.
- When inviting journalists, photographers or film crew to an event, provide written details well in advance to enable the facilities to be scheduled. Confirm their attendance and follow up with a reminder call a few days prior.
- Know how the information can best reach the right person. If possible, obtain the journalists direct phone number at work and at home, for urgent contact if necessary. Do not abuse this privilege.

Media Releases....

- Journalists receive many media releases and only exceptional ones do not get lost in the system. Ensure the stories are to the point, exciting, of widespread interest, and are explained in simple and concise terms.
- Ensure there are no mistakes in the copy and specify exact details of time, date, day and place, and who, where, when and why, in the early part of the release.
- Provide short paragraph leads with an attention grabbing headline, good quotes, anecdotes, milestones about to be achieved, statistics, tidbits and history. Emphasize the best aspects but remember that embellishments may detract from the release and discourage coverage. To increase the possibility of exposure, the angle taken in the release must match the profile of the program or publication and the particular journalist. Provide double spaced, typed copy, leaving a wide margin for editorial comments. Copy that can be used with minor editing is more likely to be run.

Photo Opportunities....

- Still photographers require good places to shoot from and good light to shoot with. Photographers should be invited to review the venue and select sites, usually both ground level and an elevated position. Other considerations are darkroom facilities, preferential parking for easy access for heavy equipment and the ability to change locations easily.

"Take an interest in the journalists' affairs, be a friend and develop empathy."

"Journalists, producers and editors work to tight deadlines."

- Television requires camera and commentating positions, productio truck, location (access for cables and power), access for support sei vices such as crew feeding, bathroom facilities, transmission links suc as microwave (small discs) and earth stations (large discs). Inquii whether an in-house feed can be provided for other media, VIP's anc video screens.

- Specify details of photo opportunities. Television footage and photc graphs speak louder than words. People always look at photograph and illustrations and read captions but do not always listen or reac copy. If it is not possible to obtain a camera crew or photographe because of prior commitments, provide broadcast quality footage fo television, publishing quality 8" X 10" black and white photograph for newspapers or color transparencies for magazines. In general, me ropolitan press will not use stock photographs, preferring to take actio or promotion shots themselves. Local press will often use supplie photographs providing they are interesting, involve action, huma interest or a personality. Ensure photos have a cardboard backing t prevent damage and do not write on the photograph as indentatior will show through. The name, title and relevance of each person in th video or photo must be clearly detailed and firmly taped to the phot or cassette. It is often worthwhile to provide television stations with color transparency as they may use it as a backdrop graphic on the screen while discussing the item.

Develop a Rapport....

- Assist the media in any way possible, provide the details of the orga nization, phone, addresses, fax and contacts at home and office fc their convenience.

- Invite the media to all briefings, or any other activity involved wit the promotion and give them a reason to attend.

- Journalists should be invited to functions. This gives them a stronge affinity with the organization.

- Support good media contacts by giving the best stories to those wh provide coverage on an ongoing basis.

At an Event....

- Provide the media with the best available tickets to the event, provid refreshments, invitations and to pre or post event functions. Remembe journalists have many alternative activities they can attend if their trea ment is unsatisfactory.

- At a major event, a media center with the following facilities should b provided: photocopier, typewriters, telex, telephones, facsimil machines, television monitors, desks and seating, rack of media release

"Remember, journalists have many alternatives if your treatment of them is unsatisfactory."

information leaflets, incident reports and notice boards. It is advisable to provide an interview room for the major media, television, radio and press. Journalists should be provided with tea, coffee, cold beverages and snacks during the event and a bar at the conclusion of the event seldom goes unrewarded.

- Where the event is being televised, feed the television picture into the media area for close-ups and replays.
- Provide updated information on any changes or late developments to journalists prior to the event and then as they occur.
- Provide security in the media area to keep out non-journalists.

Follow Up....

Everything is "on the record".

- Throughout the event, provide a regular update to local electronic media. By continuing this practice, an increasing number of stations will begin to broadcast the supplied updates.
- Immediately after the event, telex or fax highlight reports to the various media that did not attend. Media that have not traditionally provided coverage may commence to do so if they constantly receive material.
- After the event, phone and thank the journalists for their support. If no coverage was received, thank them for attending and ask if they enjoyed the presentation. Don't complain about lack of coverage. Either the story was not good enough to warrant coverage or was cut by the editor or sub-editor because of space constraints.

Other tips to assist in obtaining increased and improved coverage

- Restrict media comment to one member of the entity. This policy develops continuity and minimizes confusion.
- Everything is "on the record". It always pays to be honest and not "play games" with the media. Don't say anything, or do anything, not intended for publication.
- In television interviews, always look directly at the camera and make the sentences short and to the point. This gives the station a better opportunity to obtain a short, strong self-contained quote (grab).
- In some media organizations, editorial coverage is more readily obtained if advertising space is purchased. Allow this suggestion to come from the publication.
- Constantly source television interviews and photograph opportunities for various administrators and personalities, and ensure they wear a shirt or jacket or cap that mentions the organization/product.
- Invite media personalities, preferably those with their own program or column, to participate. This increases the likelihood of exposure.

- Obtain a small segment in a TV or radio program or a newspaper colum for a representative of the product or event.

- Interest a media outlet in running an ongoing "profile", or a contest tha will create interest, and educate the public to the product or event.

- Provide information on all activities to the Community Service Director at each of the media outlets. In many cases, exposure can be obtained at no cos

"The media has no obliga-tion to provide your product or event with exposure."

Many marketers believe the media has an obligation to provide exposur to their activity. The media has no such obligation. By observing these guide lines, a close rapport can be developed with the media, resulting in benefi for all concerned. Essentially, to maximize media exposure it is necessary to:

- Be available
- Be accurate
- Be positive
- Be honest
- Be on the telephone

Stationery and Newsletters

Some 20 years ago, I was told by a successful businessman that *"if you stic 1,000 letterheads on the wall and yours does not stand out from the rest, it is sim ply not good enough."* Experience has found this to be a good philosophy.

Letterheads, business cards and other stationery form the initial imag of a business. If they are shabby, the impression conveyed is shabby; if the sta tionery is fun, the image of the business is fun. Stationery should convey th image the entity wishes to impart to the community.

"If you stick 1,000 letter-heads on the wall and yours does not stand out from the rest, it is simply not good enough."

All stationery should display the entity's name and logos, whic should reflect the corporation or organizations dynamism, nature and co ors, in a practical, simple and easily identifiable way. When designing logo, it must be remembered that conveying the entity's image is mor important than creating an artistic masterpiece. The stationery must als contain:

- Street address (including post code)
- Postal address (including post code)
- Phone number (including prefix)
- Telex number
- Fax number
- E-mail details
- World Wide Web Universal resource locator (U.R.L.)

If the entity has a patron or an advisory panel and they are well known and respected, the inclusion of their names on the letterhead will add prestige to the organization. If the company has been established for quite some time it will also prove beneficial to include the "established in xxxx" or "A part of your business since xxxx" this will reflect stability, honesty and respectability.

Once the theme and appropriate color scheme is established, this is extended through all stationery, including:

- Letterheads

- Business cards

- With Compliments slips

- Envelopes

- Invoice forms

When seeking support from the public, politicians and sponsors, the image of the stationery may contribute to their decision. Stationery that projects the impression of a professional organization enhances the opportunities.

Media Release Forms

Journalists receive such a wealth of written material that it is important to ensure media releases create a favorable impression and are easily located amongst other paper work. Media release forms contain all the elements included in the stationery but should have an identifying feature such as a brightly colored strip reading "Media Release" down the side. The name and business and private phone numbers of the organization's media contact should also be included on the form.

The Raiders media release letterhead is effective in gaining the attention of journalists.

Selecting a Public Relations Agency

The P.R. agent of most benefit will develop and place stories that build an empathy and a relationship between the public, the product/activity and its personalities. This requires a unique ability.

"Stationery that projects professionalism enhances opportunities."

The Role of a Public Relations Agency....

The normal scope of public relations companies includes preparir briefs for journalists, issuing media releases, organizing and supplying gue lists for promotional functions and constantly seeking publicity through cr ative ideas. Sourcing mailing lists of target groups for promotional/adve tising drives and public appearances is also a function of public relations.

Locating an Agency....

The best way to locate the most effective representative is to contact jou nalists in the various media and find out who they respect and trust. Anoth is to check client lists to determine the agencies who specialize in products a similar nature, and obtain references from these clients. Frequently, the pri cipal requirement is regional P.R. and it is advantageous to select a local grou with the capacity to address national media as required. After determining short list, a visit to their offices will reveal the calibre of their staff, equipmer general organization and efficiency. The size of the agency is not relevant, it the empathy with the person who will work on the account, their enthusias and the quality of their backup that is important.

One of the benefits of engaging a public relations company is to cap talize on their rapport with journalists, and consequently the personalit confidence and integrity of the account executive is critical in the selection

Select a Listener....

"An agency that has instant solutions to address the marketers requirements, should not be selected."

P.R. is frequently the communication of a message which address research findings for specific target markets. Therefore, it is important th the P.R. company is prepared to take time to understand the aims, ambition research data and strategies of the marketer. An agency that professes in tr first briefing to understanding the particular product industry, or has insta solutions to address the marketers requirements, should not be selected.

The Cost....

Essentially, P.R. firms are paid for the time spent on the account wit travel, production and out-of-pocket expenses such as couriers, photocopyir and entertainment charged at cost plus 5-15%. The industry rule of thumb that approximately 35% of each dollar paid to the agency should go direct on salaries and associated benefits. Some agencies only accept clients on twelve month contract while others will accept project clients. Most agenci charge a minimum monthly fee which includes a specified number of ma hours with additional hours charged at an hourly rate. When retaining a agency, it is customary to pay the first and last months retainer plus a advance against expenses.

What the Agency Provides....

The agency will appoint an account executive to work directly with, and always be accessible to, the client. The client should be briefed each week by the account executive on initiatives undertaken on their behalf by the agency and each month this review of accomplishments and a forecast of the upcoming months program should be examined with company principals.

The Role of a Public Relations Agency....

The normal scope of public relations companies includes preparing briefs for journalists, issuing media releases, organizing and supplying guest lists for promotional functions and constantly seeking publicity through creative ideas. Sourcing mailing lists of target groups for marketing drives and public appearances is also a function of public relations. The account executive should be involved with the organization's marketing planning meetings in order to be fully conversant with strategies and to advise on the P.R. potential of various programs.

Assessing Performance

It is impossible to measure P.R. performance quantitatively as the number of stories obtained is dependent to a large degree on the popularity and size of the client. It is much more difficult to place an effective story for a small entity, however, the benefit derived from it may be significantly more important than the same exposure for a major organization. The measure is in the quality and placement of effective stories, media attendance at conferences or briefings, attention to follow up with copy, photographs and footage and the endeavor of the agency.

The measure of performance is in the quality and placement of effective stories."

6 Sales Promotion

In today's environment it is important to maximize the use of marketing tools which not only deliver cost effective communication but provide both benefits and incentives to committed and potential consumers.

As a result of fierce competition from an increasing number of like products and other alternatives, the public's loyalty vacillates, depending on the benefits being communicated. Decision making at the point of purchase is also increasing rapidly. In 1970, only 7% of purchase decisions were made at the store, in 1995 that percentage had increased to 65%.

Decline in Brand Loyalty

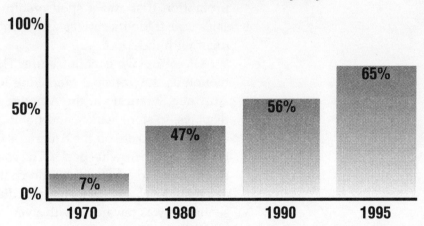

% of Purchase Decisions Made at Store

As a result, sales promotion has become an integral part of the marketing mix and takes over where advertising leaves off. A very simple definition says *"Advertising changes attitudes, sales promotion changes behavior."* Advertising creates positioning and generates public awareness of the product. This is where sales promotion begins. Sales promotion is the sharp end of advertising, extending the marketing and, by its own definition, addressing specific sales objectives. This chapter provides a broad perspective on the application of the most popular sales-promotion techniques. To effectively utilize sales promotion as a marketing tool, it is necessary to understand the benefits each technique can deliver and in what circumstance each should be applied.

"Advertising changes attitudes, sales promotion changes behavior."

The Rapid Growth of Sales Promotion

Sales promotion spending is increasing dramatically as highly sophist cated targeting enables the results of a promotion campaign to be measured cost per sale, as against cost per thousand impacts with traditional advertisin

In the United States, the amount of money committed to sales promotio greatly exceeds the expenditure on direct advertising. Sales promotio expenditure has been growing at 7-20% per annum since the early 1980' while advertising budgets have been either stagnating or, at best, growir slowly in real terms.

Sales Promotions Magnify Involvement and Enhance Potential

Frequently, corporations utilize event association for sales promo tions. They use an asset they see as being valuable, i.e. the event entity, carry their name or brand to consumers through media exposure, promo tion and direct involvement at the events. Wheat Thins sponsorship of criterium bicycle races in major American cities was designed to capitaliz on the rapidly growing popularity of cycling following the United State sweep at the Olympics. For Wheat Thins, this represented a consumer sal promotion first and a sponsorship of bike races second. They regarde sales and trade incentives as the most important aspect of their involv ment with the sport.

Premium wine manufacturer Thomas Hardy and Sons, used sales pr motion as the principal marketing tool to support sponsorship of the S Australia Syndicate in the America's Cup. Thomas Hardy used extensiv displays, in-store leaflets and point-of-sale material to offer consumers tl opportunity to attend the America's Cup on a luxury cruise ship with ever purchase of their wine packs. The company invoked Australians nationali tic emotions to effectively reinforce their sponsorship of the America's Cu at a retail level while encouraging direct sale of their product. This patriot sentiment was rewarded with a very successful promotion and record sale In addition, the company was able to distinguish its sponsorship in the pul lic's mind from the plethora of sponsors who were touting America's Cu association. Sales and trade incentives enhance the sponsors position at bo the distributor and retail level where they increase the sales and prof potential. The point-of-sale material attracts the consumer to the produ and generates a purchase.

Cutting Through the Clutter

Advertising requires repeated exposure to be effective. The fragme tation of the media is making it increasingly more difficult and less co effective for corporations to obtain the high brand awareness previous available through repeated advertising exposure.

"The point of sale material attracts the consumer and generates a purchase."

"Advertising requires repeated exposure to be effective. Sales promotion can motivate a consumer on the 'spot'".

It will become increasingly important to motivate a consumer to action in the post advertising phase as it becomes increasingly difficult to make repeated contact with that consumer through fragmented media.

Association with an event creates the opportunity to enhance the appeal of the product at the point of sale where over 60% of all purchase decisions are made. Repeated research has shown the public's strong association with particular events, personalities and athletes results in support for companies affiliated with 'their' event.

Devising a Promotion Takes Time

A nine to twelve month lead up time is required to devise on effective tie-in promotion. From initiation of contact with the potential partner to getting an agreement signed can take up to 3 months, 1 month for development of the creative, 2 months to produce promotion materials with an additional 3 months required to execute details of the promotion.

Summary

Sales promotions may be used to create awareness, to motivate and to stimulate the public to buy or to buy more often. They provide a focus to the corporations sales teams in addition to providing them with something new to say, a new angle to work with. Sales promotions also provide a strong communication point for the general advertising campaign.

The high cost of producing television commercials and increased media fragmentation causes many advertisers to amortize costs by running the advertisements for a much longer period. This decreases the effectiveness and newness of the advertisement. On the other hand, a sales promotion running over a sustainable period maintains participant interest.

Another significant advantage of sales-promotion is that no other marketing activity, with the exception of direct response, is instantly measurable against the objectives set.

Promotional Techniques:

The selection of a promotional technique to achieve a specific objective is determined by the nature of the challenge and the results of research which identifies the various 'hot buttons' in each of the various demographics across the event's target market.

These various techniques can be utilized cost efficiently to promote the product, encourage secondary purchases, create promotional opportunities, attract new consumers and assist existing consumers to obtain more benefits from their product purchase.

It will become increasingly important to motivate a consumer to action in the post advertising phase."

Sales promotions may be used to create awareness, to motive and to stimulate the public to buy or to buy more often."

No other marketing activity, with the exception of direct response, is instantly measurable against the objectives set."

Listed below are the sales promotion tools I have found most effective;

1. Promotion - Television
2. Couponing
3. Cash Refunds
4. Sales Incentives
5. Free Premium
6. Self Liquidating Premiums
7. Dealer Incentives
8. Dealer Hospitality
9. Promotion - Radio
10. Point of Sale Displays
11. Special Packs
12. Continuity Premiums
13. Sweepstakes/Contests
14. Telepromotions
15. Sampling
16. Press Promotion
17. Caused Related

"Couponing produces a continued sales increase after the expiration of the offer."

The following provides a brief explanation of each of these effective marketing tools and how the particular technique can work for a corporation.

1. **Television:** There is no doubt that television is the most effective communication medium. Television conveys sound, action, color, light, emotion movement, excitement and information. Sales promotions on television ca most effectively convey the excitement of the promotion and tie-it into t emotion, the fun, the roar of the crowd and the smell of the grease paint o a one-to-one basis with every viewer.

2. **Couponing:** Couponing has had a dramatic effect on traditional advertising as it enables an immediate and measurable response while retaing the ability to be specifically targeted.

    The effectiveness of couponing varies depending on the method coupon distribution, the popularity of the product, and the face value the coupon. Research is required to determine the most appropriate off and method of distribution that will reach the largest number of poter ially interested recipients.

    Scanner Sales Data in Washington, D.C. recently studied the sales pe formance of 11 categories of products couponed over a 6 week perio The results were significant.

Coupon Distribution period(6 wks)	Coupon Expiration period(12wks)	Coupon Post period	Average All periods
Sales Increase +19%	+30%	+23%	+24%

While couponing produces a significant increase in sales at the time of the promotion, the most important factor is the continued sales increase after the expiration of the offer due to repurchasing by people who were introduced to the product by the promotion.

Coupons are important as a marketing tool because they provide one of the most important resources of all, a database.

Cross couponing can also be extremely effective. For example, providing a coupon for a discount on merchandise or another product with each purchase provide a strong buying incentive.

Remember, couponing was never intended to be a substitute for advertising and promotion, it is to be used in conjunction with the main marketing thrust. The advantage of couponing is that at all times the bottom line relationship between cost and return is readily determinable.

3. **Cash Refunds:** Despite the "plastic money society," people love to have cash in their pockets. People regard paying for an item by check or credit card differently to spending cash. To receive cash-back in their hand is a big incentive.

4. **Sales Incentive:** Usually in the form of buy one get one free discounting (such as 25% off), and Red Spot specials, this technique enjoys many applications. Discount prices on merchandise (particularly slow moving stock), motivation to purchase new products, incentives to specific demographics are all applications for sales incentives.

A variation on the "sales" incentive is the purchase incentive. In 1988, Visa, Citibank and the NFL created an NFL affinity card which features the logos, helmets and colors of the NFL teams. Citibank attracted new card holders by appealing to their interest in the NFL teams and provided them with discounts on NFL catalog merchandise and free merchandise based on the extent of their card use. NFL properties, the marketing arm of the NFL, receives a percentage of the sales and a share of the annual card fees and interest collected on card payments.

> **"Coupons provide one of the most important resources of all, a database."**

**Kick off the fun.
Sign with your favorite team and earn money-saving bonuses towards NFL gear.**

"Negotiating premium positions in the retailers advertising, end of aisle or window displays is an effective method of increasing market share."

5. **Free Premiums:** The attachment of a benefit not usually related directly to the product in order to generate sales is called a free premium offer. An example is Wranglers provision of a free rodeo ticket for each pair of jeans purchased. This premium addressed the target market and reinforced Wrangler's sponsorship involvement in rodeo.

    Premiums can be used to excite people, increase coupon redemption, and encourage multiple purchases. Premium giveaways, where the consumer needs to collect a number of proof of purchase are also popular.

6. **Self Liquidating Premiums:** This is the attachment of a benefit generally not related to the product which the purchaser buys at a bargain price, usually only slightly more than the item's production cost.

    This marketing tool can be used as reinforcement for consumers or as an additional incentive to entice new people to purchase. For example, a $9.99 item of merchandise offered for $4.99 with every item purchased is an effective promotion.

    If the premium is unrelated to the product, the marketer can negotiate special prices in return for the advertising and promotion provided to the supplier.

7. **Dealer Incentives:** Promotions aimed at convincing the distributors or retailers to promote the product in preference to other alternatives may include:

    - Instituting an advertising and/or promotional campaign to support the dealer or retailer.
    - Various sales promotions and personality appearances to support sales.
    - Improved margins for the retailer.
    - Offering hospitality opportunities.
    - Increased market share for the retailer.

"Dealer incentives enhance the dealers enthusiasm for the promotion".

These measures enhance the dealer's enthusiasm for the event or product.

Negotiating premium positions in the retailers advertising, end of aisle or window displays in exchange for promotional and advertising support or increased margins is an effective method of increasing market share.

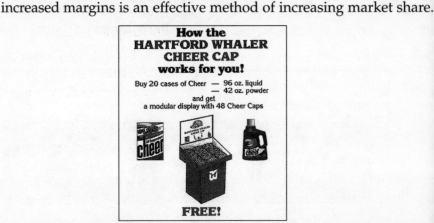

Material Courtesy of National Hockey League

This N.H.L. promotion provides retailers of Cheer detergent with a modular display and 48 Hartford Whaler Cheer caps with a purchase of 20 cases of Cheer.

8. **Hospitality:** Hospitality is a key sales weapon and the marketer can utilize an event to entertain existing or potential clients in a relaxed environment, establish a one-on-one relationship and develop an improved understanding. Hospitality produces a feeling of obligation in the mind of the guest, which creates increased leverage for an ongoing business commitment.

> "Hospitality creates increased leverage for an ongoing business commitment."

9. **Radio Promotion:** Radio is a very effective medium for promotion because, particularly at Breakfast (usually 6-9 a.m.) and Drive (4-7p.m.) when the majority of the public are driving to or from work, it reaches a captive market.

    Radio is a communication medium that allows a high frequency due to its relatively low cost and narrower targeting than television. This enables target audience reach without huge message spill. Radio is also more flexible in its programming than television and can therefore fulfill promotional needs without requiring a large support advertising schedule.

> "Radio enables target audience reach without huge message spill."

10. **Point of Sale Displays:** The establishment of a special display at the retail or wholesale outlet can take many forms. Particularly effective was a program we instituted for Johnson & Johnson featuring life-size cut-outs of Australia's test cricket captain which were set up in every supermarket in Australia during the cricket season. The promotion, which offered purchase incentives in addition to a consumer competition, achieved excellent sales results and attracted customer attention to the captain, the Australian team and the game itself. The effectiveness of this promotion technique was greatly enhanced by tying back the point of sale displays to additional promotional activities, such as couponing, TV, radio, and magazine promotion. This increased the overall promotional reach and impact in addition to providing strong positive sponsor message reinforcement at retail level.

    For Point of Purchase to be successful, it must be:

    • Informing, reminding, persuading and merchandising.

    The display must:

    • Be eye catching, conserve space, increase profitability for the retailer.
    • Have the product as the central focus, tie in with other ads, clearly describe the competition or promotion.

11. **Special Packs:** Either the marketer alone, or in conjuction with an event produces commemorative merchandise, star personalities or picture packs, to set the product apart from its' competition and even enhance the regular appearance of the merchandise. If an event is involved, this packaging attracts the supporters of the event to buy a souvenir. To maximize their effectiveness, special packs should be introduced for a short period of time and have direct relevance to the event or promotion.

12. **Continuity Premiums:** A selection of items, such as individual player medallions, trading cards or posters, are produced in sets and customers are offered each piece in the set over a certain period of time.

13. **Sweepstakes/Contests:** Sweepstakes and contests are extremely popular because everyone loves to win. Generally, to enter a sweepstakes it is necessary to obtain a coupon contained on the packaging of the product. Therefore, in order to enter the sweepstakes, it is necessary to purchase the product. In some parts of Australia, Europe and the United States, conditional sweepstakes are illegal, meaning that purchasing the product cannot be a condition of entry into the competition. In this situation an alternative source of obtaining coupons must be available.

    Two successful examples of sweepstakes were those held by Gillette and ESPN. Gillette's consumer sweepstakes in retail stores, gave American football fans a chance to win $50,000 and 2 lifetime passes to the Super Bowl. Consumers completed an entry form nominating who they thought would win their league's MVP Award. Promotion material contained in a free-standing insert distributed to 40 million homes across America directed consumers to retail stores for entry blanks and also included a refund offer on participating Gillette products.

    The ESPN World Tour Sweepstakes included prime seat tickets to four major international events, the Brazilian Grand Prix in Rio de Janeiro, the French Open Tennis tournament in Paris, the British Open Golf championship in Scotland, and the Italian Grand Prix in Monza. Pan-Am provided airline tickets for the winners and consequently the promotion was geared to Pan-Am's European and South American destinations. In return Pan-Am received 15 second inserts in all of the 60 second Sweepstakes commercials featured on ESPN.

    This promotion worked for the events by providing excellent promotion and exposure; it worked for Pan-Am as the sponsor; and it positioned ESPN as 'the' sports network.

14. **Telepromotions:** The telepromotion industry is a new, but rapidly growing marketing tool. The use of free and premium calls (800 and 900 numbers) are being increasingly used by major corporations. The Coca-Cola Halloween promotion for the NFL offered consumers prizes for calling an 800 number and keying in "Monster Code" numbers found on specially marked multipacks of Coke products. In just five weeks the promotion generated 32 million phone calls from consumers.

15. **Sampling:** People generally purchase products they have grown up with. In addition, a large percentage of people do not feel strongly about any particular product. To overcome any resistance due to lack of knowledge or interest and to encourage a 'give it a try' attitude, sampling can be effective.

16. **Press Promotion:** For most products or event organizations, the clutter in newspaper advertising reduces the cost effectiveness of a sales promotion unless the advertisement is substantial (which is expensive) or the newspaper or magazine gets behind the promotion with front or back page pointers or editorial. Newspaper promotion for most products is acceptable because in most cases a "flat product" is being sold. Events however, are an emotive purchase and unless the supporting campaign is extremely creative, newspaper advertising is less effective than an emotive media such as television or radio. Cross promotions, in which another medium such as radio highlights the newspaper promotion, can enhance the promotion by increasing the awareness and enabling the radio to hype the concept of the promotion while the newspaper provides the details.

17. **Cause Related:** This form of promotion allows the marketer to take advantage of the goodwill engendered by the cause involved in the promotion. The sponsor donates a percentage of the sales resulting from the promotion to the cause as an incentive for people to purchase. An excellent example was the Visa Card Olympic promotion. This program encouraged consumers to make contributions to the U.S. Olympic team by making credit card purchases. Visa ran three fund raising programs which raised over $2 million for the U.S. Olympic team.

The **Visa Transaction Program** contributed a specified amount to the Olympic team every time the Visa card was used for a purchase.

The **Visa Card Issuing Program** provided member institutions with the opportunity to issue both new and renewal Visa cards bearing the Visa Olympic logo reinforcing the promotion to consumers.

The **Visa Direct Donation Program** allowed card holders to make direct contributions to the U.S. Olympic team through Visa monthly statement inserts. The use of Visa card and travellers checks to directly benefit the Olympians resulted in greatly increased card usage.

The gas station stamped a base with each purchase of 15 litres of motor fuel. Each base stamped represented a discount at McDonalds and cash for Youth Amateur Baseball.

*Barry's Camera & Video
Promotion*

Summary

Sales promotion techniques are a very important aspect of any marketing endeavor. Sales Promotion is also the tool by which the marketer differentiates their product and to maximize the benefits sales promotion can provide it is essential to understand each technique and it's application.

Examples of Sales Promotions:

To provide the inspiration to develop sales promotions that generate public interest, motivation, participation and which result in sales, a number of simplified examples are outlined in this section.

Far West Federal Bank

The Far West Federal Bank, competing in the market with two giant competitors, became the exclusive distributor of Portland Trailblazer schedule cards. Inside each schedule card was a $5.00 check, valid when an account for a minimum of $200.00 was opened. The schedule cards promotion resulted in increased awareness of the Far West Federal Bank and generated a staggering $13 million in new deposits.

Jewel Food Stores

Jewel produced 48 pins, one for each Olympic event and four commemorative issues, and released them three per week. Consumers could obtain them for $1.99 each without purchase or $0.99 cents each with a coupon and the purchase of designated products. The USOC received 16.5 cents for each pin sold. Brands invested incremental dollars to become a designated product.

Barry's Camera and Video

Official entry forms to the Barry's Dallas Cowboys "Photographer of the Game" competition are published in the Dallas Times Herald and people must register at any Barry's Camera and Video Store. The winner receives a sideline photographers pass, the use of professional camera equipment and additional benefits provided by the team at the event.

Campbell's Soup

Campbells Soup sponsorship of the extremely successful Christmas Spectacular at Radio City Music Hall provided for a $5.00 discount off the regular ticket price in exchange for five soup labels. Campbells promoted the event in all advertising and the "Campbell Kids" were included in the shows advertising campaign.

Sheraton Plaza La Reina

The Zeno's bar at the Sheraton Hotel offered wide screen TV coverage of Monday Night Football, prizes including a trip for two to the Super Bowl and a half time question and answer analysis by a member of the Los Angeles Raiders. The result, a very crowded bar and record sales.

Maxwell House Coffee

Maxwell House reinforced its sponsorship of a Winston Cup team by touring a simulator racing car through malls and food stalls. Consumers with proof of purchase were invited to drive in a simulated stock car race.

Gillette

The promotion gets consumers to watch sponsored NASCAR races and awards prizes to consumers who can identify the race leader at the halfway point. To qualify, consumers must call a 900 number during the race and leave their name and telephone number. The call costs 95 cents. Within thirty minutes of the halfway lap, some consumers are called back and if they can correctly identify the driver they win prizes ranging from Chevrolet cars to Gillette merchandise and product. The promotion receives up to half a million calls per race.

Geo Motor Vehicle

Research showed potential Geo buyers to be environmentally conscious so to reinforce the cars rating as the most fuel efficient vehicle in the United States, the company sponsored a number of environmental activities. Geo planted a tree for every person buying a Geo vehicle or attending a Geo sponsored event. This promotion positioned Geo as a responsible citizen to its target market.

Phillips Lighting Company

Using the theme "Phillips National Night Out will help lower the crime rate," this promotion encouraged homeowners to turn on outside lights and spend time outdoors with neighbors. The Phillips National Night Out Cup was awarded to the community with the most successful event. Consumer sales support included promotional materials, home security kits and in- store displays with McGruff the Crime Dog. The company contributed to anti-crime organizations for every Longer Lite bulb sold. The industrial/commercial sector of the Phillips sales force worked with local National Night Out projects such as parades, barbecues etc. which developed their relationship with the local utility companies.

Books & Company

This sponsorship included a "Meet the Orchestra" program for pre-schoolers, a learn-to-conduct session, tickets and hospitality benefits. The store gave a donation of 20% to the orchestra in return for its promotion of Books and Company gift certificates in newsletters, programs and mailings.

Elliotts Juices

The company placed the event logo on the label of 50,000 bottles and included literary quotes on the inside of its bottle caps as part of its cross promotional sponsorship of a childrens expo.

Motts USA

The Motts Reading Program, advertised in free standing inserts across the United States, used reading as their focus for store displays and offered children's books with proof of purchase. To reach their primary consumers, school children, the company offered free reading packs to elementary schools nationwide. These packs included books, book marks and stickers bearing their logo. The highlight of the program was the presentation of awards to 20 winners of the Motts essay contest and their teachers.

Summary

These few examples illustrate how marketers can extend the exposure and positioning afforded by a promotional tie-in to increase the reach and frequency of this investment and directly enhance sales opportunities.

In the majority of instances, if the marketer has not used the various available techniques to obtain value for the investment prior to the event or activity occurring, the involvement has not been correctly implemented. It is therefore in the best interest of both the tie-in and the marketer to develop sales promotions to increase the benefits of both parties.

"If the marketer has not obtained value for the investment prior to the event the involvement has not been correctly implemented."

Chapter 7 Promotions

The Webster's Dictionary definition of promotion is "to incite or urge a person to do something." A promotion can also be described as "an event designed to stimulate or change behavior by the use of incentive."

The general public has a profusion of products available to them and advertising creates an awareness of these. Promotions accentuate and boost that awareness, providing the incentive needed for people to commit to one in preference to another. The advantage promotions enjoy over general advertising is their ability to solicit participation which creates an emotional interaction with the potential client and entices their involvement and commitment.

Similar principles apply to both promotion and advertising. In order to stage a successful promotion, it is essential to know and understand the attitudes of the various market segments i.e., to know what will motivate the demographic being solicited to a particular product. The promotion must be relevant, possess strong target market appeal and be integrated with the overall marketing and advertising strategy. If the product is an event it should compliment the event sponsor's involvement. An example of specific promotion event targeting was the NBA drive, in conjunction with a series of corporate sponsors, for more female fans. The NBA operated a tour of shopping malls throughout the United States to demonstrate elements of the game specifically to women. Each exhibit was sponsored by a different company and endorsed by leading household-name players. The players demonstrated a range of skills, many involving the public competing for prizes. The shoppers could also have their photographs taken with realistic life-size cutouts of these giant athletes. A continuous video featured a selection of highlights of the more remarkable passages of play.

The concept of the promotion was to create an appreciation of the degree of difficulty involved in basketball, and emphasize the size, athleticism and remarkable skills of the players. The promotion was extremely successful, creating a greater awareness of professional basketball among women. The sponsors provided product or merchandise for prizes, reinforcing their tie-in with the NBA.

Promotions should involve the corporation or organizations marketing and promotional departments as well as their advertising, public relations and promotion agencies. Each should provide creative input and marketing assistance.

Promotions accentuate and boost awareness, providing the incentive needed for people to commit "

The promotion must be relevant, possess strong target market appeal and be integrated with the overall marketing and advertising strategy."

It is invariably good business sense for promotions to create a positiv community image and avoid exposure, product association and concep that may have a down side risk. Prior to implementation, promotior should be fully thought out and developed.

To maximize the benefits of a promotion, the following steps should be fo lowed:

In the first step the desired end result should be clearly understoo defined and articulated. It is frequently possible to achieve several objectiv in a single creative promotion. These may include:

- Achievement of a specific marketing goal.
- Increased general awareness.
- Positive community image.
- Free media exposure.
- Specific demographic targeting.
- Motivation of members/employees/trade.

A think-tank, comprising the corporate marketers and their variou agencies, determine concepts that may achieve the specified objectives. Tl feasibility of each is researched and detailed. The concepts with the poter tial to achieve the specific goals, promote the product, generate exposur appeal to the target demographic, attract media attention and support tl overall marketing strategy are selected for further evaluation.

"The objectives of the promotion are reviewed to ensure consistency with the marketing strategy."

The objectives of the promotion are reviewed to ensure consistenc with the marketing strategy. If an event is involved, the promotion mu work for both the event and the sponsor.

The potential as a promotion or competition involving a no cost med partner is evaluated. The nature of the promotion and the target market wi determine the specific media vehicle(s) that may be interested. The prome tion concept is massaged and enhanced to develop the 'hook' that max mizes its appeal to the preferred media vehicle. For many small project local newspapers are an excellent source of promotional support.

An attention grabbing theme, reinforcing the U.S.P. is created to higl light the promotion and reinforce the overall marketing strategy.

One of the strongest personal motivations is greed and promotions a usually incentive based to maximize public interest and involvement. Tl prize selection is therefore important in many promotions. Where appropr ate, the organization, its sponsor or affiliated partner's products and ever related items should be utilized as prizes. If the promotion is created aroun an event, either by the event organization, or by a corporation using tl association, the provision of tickets as the prize also reinforces the even stature and desirability.

Where media support for the promotion is not available, other possib avenues of communication are investigated. For an event, encouragement members, season ticket holders, supporters and sponsor's employees involve their friends and associates is one starting point. Creating a spons driven promotion supported by paid media is another. Additional exposure opportunities include posters, flyers, and promotional activities held at shopping malls, beaches and other high traffic areas.

Experience suggests that providing incentives to those engaged in executing the promotion is an excellent motivator which enhances results.

By following these guidelines and ensuring that all elements of the promotion are fully considered, an excellent marketing tool can be created.

Promotion Planning

Before a promotion can be created and executed, it is important to establish the infrastructure that will enhance the calibre of the promotion, ensure effective implementation and maximize its exposure and performance.

Promotions, publicity and advertising, while being different marketing techniques, are nevertheless interrelated. It is advantageous for each to be separately implemented while being part of an umbrella strategy. This allows each discipline to be fully extended while ensuring the individual activities complement and reinforce each other and respect the overall marketing strategy.

To conduct effective promotions it is necessary to:

- Develop a thorough knowledge of the target market and the organization's overall marketing philosophy.
- Understand the objectives of any current advertising campaign.
- Have a working knowledge of the media, its personnel and its operations.
- Maintain a close liaison between the marketer and their advertising and public relations agencies.

Develop A Mailing List

A substantial number of organizations/corporations cannot attract, or afford, sufficient media support to achieve their desired objectives and therefore require alternative cost effective communication mediums. The motivation of people who are associated with, or who have indicated an interest in, the product/organization/event is such a medium. The Pittsburgh Pirates for example, have a mailing list of over 260,000 people interested in the team and its activities. Categorizing lists by degree of interest, age, sex, family structure and location, enables specific targeting for particular types of promotions and a maximization of cost effectiveness.

Wherever possible, promotions should involve the solicitation, through coupons, entry forms or telepromotions, which obtain the names, addresses and phone numbers of participants. This creates a data base of interested people which will become an extremely valuable long term asset.

"Before a promotion can be created and executed, the infrastructure must be established."

"A data base will become an extremely valuable long term asset."

Four Types of Promotions:

The purpose of a promotion is to create an incentive for people to support a particular event, product or activity in any number of ways. Essentially, promotions fall into one of the following categories;

- To achieve a specific short term goal.
- To increase overall brand, benefit and/or media awareness.
- To alter the image of the event or product.
- To generate revenue.

Promotions To Achieve A Specific Short Term Goal

While promotions may be used to achieve many short term objectives by far the most common is to increase event attendance or achieve increased market share.

Promotions can be utilized to address a weakness in a specific market or to change consumer support and preference. Promotions are valuable in areas where weakness in support may be corrected most readily.

To maximize the results of a public motivated by a promotion, it is essential to provide immediate access to the product, tickets to the event or, in a political campaign to the candidate. Promotions should provide a winning result for all of the participants.

The Tennessee Performing Arts Center (TPAC) tied McDonald's Restaurants into their Family Series by donating $1.00 to Ronald McDonald House for every ticket sold in return for exposure on the tray liners. The combination of McDonald's 90,000 customers each day and a cross promotion with radio and television meant a win-win situation. James Randolph, president of the TPAC said "We got free advertising from McDonald's, Ronald McDonald House got money and radio and television had a promotion for their stations. Everybody got something out of it."

People love to win and promotions that offer prizes will normally be well supported. Prizes of motor vehicles and world trips certainly attract the public's attention but huge prizes are usually not essential. Unusual or highly desirable prizes and incentives also attract people's attention. A gate promotion at a motorcross event which offers $2.00 off the admission price may obtain only a fraction of the support a "$2.00 off a compact disc with every full price ticket" offer will receive. The consumer saves $2.00 in both instances yet one prize may be perceived as having much greater appeal. Also, prizes that people can easily relate to, for example, keep all they can gather in a supermarket in three minutes, or pay credit card accounts to a certain value, are also very popular.

Promotion To Increase Overall Public And/Or Media Awareness

Promotions that while not focusing on a specific short term goal, create a continuing media and public profile which contributes to the product or events overall image, positioning and performance are also valuable.

> "Promotions should provide a winning result for all of the participants."

One of our clients, the 72 piece New American Orchestra, required a promotion to increase its' awareness in the community. Being cognizant of the similarity between the orchestras audience demographics and that of cycling, the countries most popular recreational sport, led to the development of the unique "Rhapsody on Wheels' promotion. This promotion featured a 20 mile recreational fun bike ride punctuated by five "musical stops" where groups of orchestra members played "clues" to enable participants to complete a musical quiz. At the conclusion of the ride the orchestra performed a free concert in the park. The uniqueness of the event generated extensive publicity and participation, each of the musical stops and the free concert attracted substantial crowds of spectators (potential supporters) and the event portrayed the orchestra in an extremely positive manner.

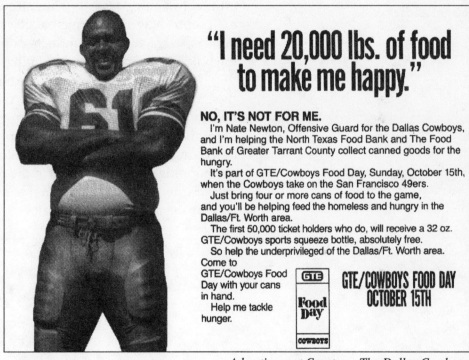

Advertisement Courtesy: The Dallas Cowboys

Food Day is a proven attendance increasing promotion with substantial community relations benefits.

To Alter The Image Of The Product or Event

Promotions and public relations are two of the most effective mediums for overcoming a negative image or to alter purchase patterns. In many instances, a sudden change in the presentation or marketing of an event or product to attract a demographic essential to long term success may result in the alienation of current consumers. Promotions allow a change or modification of image to be introduced in a highly targeted manner at a controlled pace and a cost significantly less than traditional media advertising would allow.

Promotions allow a change or modification of image at a cost significantly less than traditional media advertising."

Shopping Mall Promotions

As the public's focus on major community shopping malls increase
so does the provision of services, amenities and attractions offered by th
malls to further enhance their appeal. Neilson surveys show individua
mall attendances range between 20,000 and 80,000 people each day wit
the period of time per visit increasing each year. In the United States, ove
65% of the population attend a shopping mall each week. Of thes
approximately 70% are women who frequently attend with children.

These attendance figures and growth patterns have made shoppin
malls a very important promotional venue for products and activities. Th
provision of an interesting, entertaining presentation can result in the pro
motion becoming a focal point, attracting a huge captive audience to th
mall centre stage. The principal objective of many shopping mall promo
tions is to enhance the products popularity among women and increas
the potential to influence the families purchase decisions.

The first step is to identify the shopping malls and plazas that attrac
the target audience. For a product with an appeal across the whole com
munity it is essential to focus on those which reach the most people
Promotions to a specific demographic may require a selection proces
based on criteria more appropriate to the target market. A detailed list o
all shopping malls and plazas in the catchment area, their attendee profil
and traffic flow patterns can be obtained from center management
and/or the appropriate authorities.

> **"Identify the shopping malls and plaza's that attract the target audience."**

Illustration Courtesy: Shopping Centre Networ

The Goodwill Games Shopping Mall Tour was designed to be supported by sponsorship.

Consumer Promotions

The key to effective promotions are creativity, relevance, and correct targeting. Halls Cough Drops sponsored a "Silent Night at the Symphony" program as part of its' campaign for cough suppressants. The drops were distributed free to symphony attendees to reduce coughing and throat clearing during performances. The result was a successful, fun promotion which benefited both the sponsor and the orchestra.

The Knudsen dairy company linked up with the Raiders to create a promotion called "Raiders Readers" which encouraged children to read and included game ticket giveaways and a library distribution of 140,000 bookmarks. The bookmarks contained a short summary of a book recommended by the profiled player. This promotion not only impacted on the children but also on their parents and educators.

"The key to effective promotions are creativity, relevance, and correct targeting."

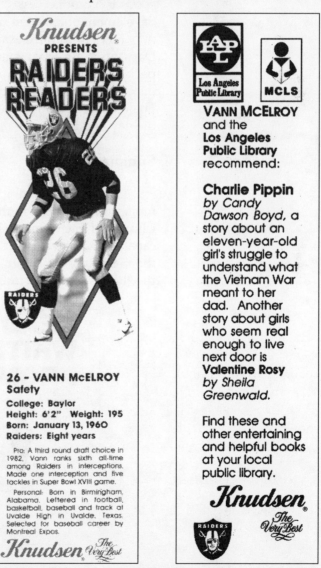

The front and back of the Raiders Bookmark encouraging children to read.

A balanced schedule of general awareness promotions and thos
intended to specifically enhance sponsor, media and consumer loyalties cre
ates not only a high profile but a measure of accessibility. This increases eac
parties identification with the event or product and its personalities an
results in a stronger long term bonding. Long term promotion strategies ca
effectively alter the image of an event or product while compatible sho
term specific promotions address immediate needs.

By working closely with its' sponsors, an event entity can obtai
valuable targeted promotion while addressing the sponsors objectives.

By working closely with a highly targeted event, corporations can ingra
tiate their products with the event supporters and achieve a number of goal:

The Amax Coal Company sponsors the "Amax A Team" promotio
where, in conjunction with local schools, good students are rewarded wit
recognition, merchandise and tickets to an Indiana Pacers NBA game. Thi
sponsor promotion assists the Pacers build loyalty among children, an esser
tial element of the teams marketing program.

Fuji Film utilize major events, festivals or parades to stage Fuji Phot
Days, often attracting many thousands of people. At each event, a Fuji valu
pack including substantial discounts off rolls of film, audio cassettes, flopp
disks, video cassettes and selected cameras is distributed to every spectato
Fuji conduct photography contests to judge the best photographs taken o
the day and booths are often set up to sell film and rent cameras.

Summary

The important point to remember is that no matter how grandiose a pro
motion may appear, in the majority of instances it is essentially the embel
ishment of one or more simple, proven ideas. Once a promotion framewor
capable of achieving the objectives is established, the elements that tie it in t
the marketing campaign, address the particular target market and provid
the "hooks" to attract public and media attention, determine its effectivenes:

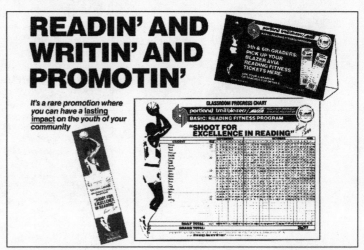

Courtesy: The Portland Trailblazers

**The Trailblazers promotional material sums it up well, "A
lasting impact on the youth of your community." An excellent
promotion.**

Chapter 8 Direct Marketing

Direct marketing is one of the fastest growing marketing disciplines. Direct marketing enables a specific message, calculated to trigger the "action button" of the potential consumer, to be delivered precisely to the target market and to be able to accurately gauge the response. Direct marketing is one of the most effective marketing and income generating tools available.

Over a period of time, on each occasion the customer makes a purchase the recorded basic demographic information can be enhanced by purchase behavior data, media preference responses and lifestyle profiles. This information is on an individual basis and not on an audience profile basis and is therefore far more targeted and accurate.

Direct marketing encompasses direct mail and direct response advertising. Direct mail is information directed specifically to a customer. Response advertising is any form of advertising response, including coupon and telephone solicitation.

There are primarily two reasons direct marketing is growing so rapidly, one is the market is becoming more quality sensitive and less price sensitive, the second is the increasing difficulty and cost of impacting the targeted consumer by traditional advertising means. .

Direct marketing began with targeting zip codes. Then came psychographics - this is how customers think about themselves and how it translates in purchases. Then synchrographics became popular- this is categorization based on lifestyle changes, such as new mothers, new retiree's, first time home buyers and so on.

Because direct marketing is such an extremely effective marketing tool it now utilizes a number of techniques almost as varied as the applications to which it can be applied. Although most products lend themselves to direct marketing, those that are creative, emotive and fun have wide public appeal that readily trigger positive responses.

There are a number of direct marketing techniques that can be effective either on their own, or as a combination.

Direct Marketing Techniques:

Telemarketing

Telemarketing is effective and popular. Telephone selling is fast, efficient and if well targeted is an extremely cost effective direct marketing technique.

If the person being contacted is already interested in the activity or product, they will usually take the phone call. If they are not available, in the majority of instances they will return the call.

Discussion of a person's lifestyle interests generates positive emotive reactions and allows a direct interaction between the salesperson and the contact. This permits the caller to excite, enthuse, address objections, adapt the presentation to fit the situation and close the sale. Importantly, the information gleaned enhances the database.

Telephone marketing is divided into inbound and outbound categories. Inbound is where replies initiated from another medium are received, a television "call the hotline" advertisement, a newspaper advertisement, and so on. Outbound is where unsolicited calls are placed to obtain a renewal or a sale.

Outbound is immediate and flexible. It can be tested quickly and inexpensively. Inbound requires research, planning and testing various formats to determine the most effective.

Provision of a telephone number in a newspaper or magazine advertisement increases responses by over 50%, so the telephone operator must be briefed and be totally au fait with the product and the benefits of the specific offer being made. The performance of the telephone operator will make or break the sale. Telephone selling is a specialist industry where the professionals research and write scripts which are continually tested and modified, where every objection is addressed. The script is totally controlled from the opening line to the close, allowing for prepared answers to a range of questions that could possibly be asked. The expert listens, evaluates and responds in a way that makes the difference between a yes and a no result.

The major benefit of telephone sales is that credit card numbers can be taken over the phone and the sale closed while the respondent is receptive and enthusiastic.

Direct Mail

The primary objectives of direct mail are to;

- Build product sales or make announcements.
- Cultivate customers, build a long term relationship.
- Support dealers or distributors by advising corporate goals or promotions.
- Personalize large corporations' communications.
- Reach potential clients in an engaging and cost effective manner.

Direct mail is simply sending a letter or brochure direct to a specific person by mail. The advantages of direct mail are:

- The message is personalized.
- The space constraints that exist in media advertising are removed.
- The replies provide the specific information being sought.
- Color, design, style and the appeal of the product can be effectively utilized to promote the objectives.
- Specialized selling and closing techniques can be employed.

"Provision of a telephone number in an advertisement increases responses by over 50%."

If the marketer does not have a qualified contact or target list, the initial use of direct mail is to determine potential customers; those individuals or corporations likely to buy the product.

To "qualify" a call means to address any questions or objections, determine whether or not the contact has a genuine interest, can afford the purchase and is likely to make a commitment, now or in the future.

Always record the overall response received by a specific promotion, not just the resultant sales. This enables evaluation of whether it is worthwhile repeating, if modifications will enhance it, the effectiveness of a follow up promotion to close additional sales and identification of the primary targets.

The cost of employing a salesman to solicit cold sales, taking into account wages, vehicle costs, overheads, insurance and the like, is in the order of $150 - $275 per call. The cost of telephone sales is approximately $5 - $10 per call when the telephone service, the sales representative, the supervisor, and overhead is included.

As a measure for comparison, a mail piece costs in the order of $0.75 - $5.00 depending on the quality of the presentation and the size of the mailing.

Direct mail advertising has many advantages;

- Selective - geographically, demographically, sociographically.
- Ideal for response - reply paid card, reply paid envelope.
- Personal - direct, no clutter, personal message.
- Format is flexible - include gifts, samples.
- Timing is flexible - time to correspond with certain events.
- Allows long copy - full explanation, ability to strategize the sale.
- Measurable.

To produce effective direct response copy the following elements are important;

- Promise benefit in the headline.
- Give assurance in the copy.
- Give benefits, benefits, benefits.
- Provide guarantees such as money back.
- Ask for the order.
- Emphasize immediate response required.
- Bonus for immediate response.

A simple way to remember what is required is to apply the PAPA formula;

- Promise.
- Amplify.
- Proof.
- Action.

For best results, make the copy one-on-one, people respond to those

Also, remember that the most read part of a letter is the P.S., so always include a P.S. and use it to close the sale, reinforce an add-on bonus for quick response or the limited time of the offer.

Other elements of an effective direct mail package include;

1. Envelope - 15% of people throw away unsolicited mail without opening. The sale must begin on the outside of envelope. It is essential to break-through the barrier of resistance.
2. Brochure - reinforce benefits, show empathy.
3. Order form - reprint all details. The only thing that should be required from the customer is the signature.
4. Act now - insert an enclosure offering a bonus for prompt reply.
5. Reply envelope - increases responses significantly.

The specific nature of each of these elements should only be determined after careful consideration and testing. The key to successful direct mail is test, test, test. Test each element individually and then each combination to ensure the best possible package.

You should also note that offers marked with important, urgent, or official are resented by over 70% of people. The effectiveness of these terms should be thoroughly analyzed before implementation.

"The most read part of a letter is the P.S."

"Offers marked with important, urgent, or official are resented by over 70% of people."

ONCE THE PITTSBURGH PIRATES TEAMED UP WITH THE POSTAL SERVICE, EVERY PITCH HIT ITS MARK.

THE PIRATES' SALES PITCH REACHED MORE FANS THAN EVER WHEN THE POSTAL SERVICE HELPED IMPROVE THE ACCURACY OF THEIR MAILING LISTS.

The Pittsburgh Pirates have focused on developing a sophisticated direct mail list which they have used to great advantage.

TV Direct Response

Television direct response is the ultimate in impulse buying. The advantages provided by television are that the excitement, ease of operation and color of the product can be conveyed to the prospective customer. The most popular employment of TV direct response are;

A. 60 second commercials. This is because;
- Advertising in off hours provides a lower ad rate.
- You can often obtain a per inquiry (PI) payment system rather than paying rack advertising rates.
- It is often possible to structure a TV station co-promotion where the station agrees to a fixed schedule and guarantees a minimum return. If this return is not obtained, the station will bonus ads until the minimum sale guarantee is met.

B. Long form ads (or infomercials) are becoming increasingly popular. In this format, the producer buys the time, usually a half hour slot, and uses this time to explain the product, provide testimonials, demonstrate the product and deliver a planned sales pitch.

C. An advertisement promoting a free video cassette which provides details of a number of offers. This is comparable to the provision of print catalogs, but with more impact.

D. Home shopping programs have enjoyed phenomenal growth and rely to a great extent on celebrity endorsements, particularly with sports products, memorabilia and fashion items.

Radio Direct Response

Radio direct response initiates an impulse call particularly when the message is delivered by respected personalities. Radio also allows message frequency.

The disadvantages are that the product is not shown, coupons cannot be provided and toll numbers cannot be flashed on the screen. This means the consumer must visualize the product and remember the phone number for ordering.

The advantage radio provides is that its audience is highly segmented. Therefore, radio direct response is usually used as a high frequency, inexpensive back up medium to supplement other advertising.

Magazines

This is a popular form of direct marketing. In direct response advertising, the CPM does not matter, the only thing that counts is the cost per order. Magazine direct response has many advantages;

- Audience selectivity - specific magazines readers have common interests and characteristics.

- Distinctive audience.
- Long shelf life - pass along readership.
- Color and quality presentation.
- More prestige than direct mail.
- Some magazines will accept PI.

In general, direct mail response is 1/2% to 5%, while magazine response is 1/2% to 2%.

Newspapers

The most common use of newspapers for direct marketing is through FSI's promoting products that can be ordered by coupon or phone.

Plastic Cards

The sending of unsolicited, prestigious looking plastic cards that entitle the bearer to a series of "benefits" has grown remarkably in recent times. This growth is a result of the greatly increased response to promotions by recipients of the cards. This is due to the perception of the cards as a prestige item affording special rights and privileges. In today's society people love to carry "plastic", making this an effective hook for a particular market segment.

Co-operative Mail

Co-operative mail provides a way to save costs. It is simply direct mail where the distribution costs are shared with another organization to either reduce mailing costs or turn mailings into a profit center. Co-operative mailing occurs either when the marketer includes a mailing piece for another party in its own mailing, or has its material inserted in another group's mailing. The latter method is called secondary mailing.

To be successful, the organization with whom your material is included must have the same or similar target audience. Providing the leaflet or brochure is a well constructed "winner," this method may produce results at considerably less than the normal cost.

On the other hand, the potential customer is being provided with alternative purchase options. The amount of money saved may be more than lost through lack of specific targeting and dilution of the message.

Of course, as we know from personal experience, if too much is received in the mail it probably won't be read. Therefore the number of mailing pieces in a co-operative mail situation should be limited, preferably to two. Another negative is the dilution of the message by the inclusion of too much information or too many offers. These factors need to be carefully weighed.

Piggy Backing

A similar technique to co-operative mailing is called piggy backing. In this technique the marketers mailing piece is enclosed with a credit card, bank statement, gas, electricity or rate account or a department store mailout

The major advantage of this method is that the mailing receives a wider reach with a document that is sure to command attention. The piggy backing entity also obtains a degree of credibility rub-off from the organization with whom the mailing is being shared. Additionally, it is more difficult psychologically to initiate a not necessary payment than it is to write a second check when paying essential accounts. By utilizing this technique in preference to co-operative mailing, the product is not competing for a sale with another organization.

The success of piggy back mailing depends on the nature of the organization the marketer is mailing with and the appeal of the offer.

This eight page mailbox drop booklet was a major contributor to the 300% increase in memberships/season tickets the team experienced in just three months. Research of 168 suburbs identified the prime target areas for distribution.

Mailbox Drops/Sampling

Mailbox drops, the distribution of non-specifically addressed material into mailboxes, have the advantage of rapid distribution to a huge number of households across a suburb or a state, either by the post office or by specialist companies.

One problem faced by mailbox deliveries is the growing aversion to "junk mail".

One problem faced by mailbox deliveries is the growing aversion to "junk mail". This, coupled with the litter problem in apartments and security high-rise buildings, can create a negative attitude towards the product.

Specialist mailbox distribution companies have highly sophisticated databases that enable exceptional targeting, even within particular streets. This enables more cost effective distribution than the Post Office which primarily distributes by zip code.

"Sampling in mail boxes is a highly effective way of "cutting through the clutter."

Sampling in mail boxes is a highly effective way of "cutting through the clutter" of products available to the consumer. In today's marketplace getting the public to try your product can be half the battle. Sampling is not inexpensive. By the time the product and a letter explaining about the product and its benefits is printed and distributed, the costs are substantial. It is therefore important to ensure delivery only to homes where there is a potential to benefit.

It is essential to test mailbox drops with a pilot sampling. If distribution to 10,000 mailboxes is planned, experiment with 50 in several locations within the target area, gauge the response, then determine whether to proceed. A response of 1- 2% for a well designed, strong project mail drop is a good result.

Combination

The use of two or more techniques to reinforce the direct marketing program can be very effective. It is not uncommon to run media advertising in conjunction with direct mail, the most usual being the combination of television or radio and mailbox drop. The broadcast campaign runs for a few days prior to the drop advising people to watch their mailbox for the special offer. One week later a follow up television or radio commercial urges people to fill in and return the response coupon and to thank people for the already "excellent response."

The major advantage of direct marketing is that after the target market has been correctly identified, the message to be communicated can be specifically crafted and directed to pre-qualified potential customers.

"The secret of successful direct marketing is to improve the marketing procedures and techniques."

Direct marketing is a technique with which the vast majority of the public is familiar and readily accept. However, as with all specialist disciplines, it is not simply a matter of couponing, phoning or sending a mail piece to a name on a list. The message must sell benefits, be short, specific, personal and well presented, constructed to overcome potential objections and appeal emotionally or egotistically.

The secret of successful direct marketing is to constantly upgrade and refine the contact list and analyze, test and improve the marketing procedures and techniques. This includes comparing different approaches, timing and formats. The approach, appearance and nature of each campaign must be different to prevent people from becoming blase. Once the appeal loses impact, the financial returns will drop dramatically.

Determining the Cost:

When ascertaining the costs of direct marketing, it is easy to overlook some important expenses that can make the exercise appear more profitable than it actually is. For example, all the following costs must be included:

Radio:

Copy writing.
Studio time for recording.
Talent fee.
Cost of audio tapes.
Radio schedule cost.
Staff cost.
Credit card costs.
Printing thank you letters.
Postage.
Couriers, photocopies, faxes, phone calls.

Direct Mail: List rental.
Artwork, typesetting.
Printing letters, brochures, postage-paid reply envelopes, response coupon envelopes.
Staff time writing material, delivery.
Personalization of letters.
Insertion costs.
Postage.
Credit card costs.
Printing thank you letters.
Couriers, photocopies, faxes, phone calls.

When preparing budgets on specific projects it is important not to overlook overhead costs. At the end of the day, the rent, the phone calls, the couriers, the labor time and other overheads have to be paid and if they were incurred as a result of a particular direct marketing project, they must be accounted for and allocated to that project.

Summary

With rapid media proliferation, market fragmentation, increasing traditional advertising cost, reduced brand loyalty and a need to personalize messages to an increasingly more cynical and analytical consumer, direct marketing will occupy a growing segment of the strategy of most marketeers in the future.

Chapter 9

Licensing And Merchandising

Logos are a valuable tool in all corners of the world.

The name of the event, sports organization or product, its logo, and the slogan and jingle created to promote it are the entities most powerful marketing tools. They identify and position the product, and are a valuable source of revenue.

The marketing industry has hundreds of examples of logos that have generated immeasurable exposure, leverage and income for their owners. Corporate names such as Pierre Cardin, Harley Davidson, the Viking helmet of the Raiders and the Wimbledon logo, are just a few examples. In fact, the range of licenses available is continuing to broaden; Forrest Gump chocolates, Nittany Lion perfume (for Penn State University), the Canadian Mounties and team mascot shaped pasta illustrate this point.

When a name or logo has the image in the community, that image can be licensed to others to enhance the appeal of their merchandise, at the same time promoting the owner of the property and generating revenue. Since the consumer is influenced as much by the license as the actual product, involving a product with established entities with high public appeal, saves the manufacturer the enormous cost of brand building.

The effectiveness of licensing and merchandising is reflected by it's growth. Product licensing expanded by 5% in 1994 to $70 billion in the United States and Canada, following a 7% gain in 1993.

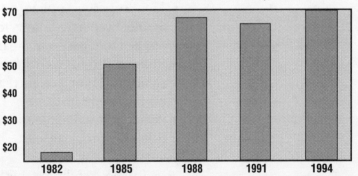

Television program, entertainment and character licensing grew by 9% while music related licenses grew 8%. Toy and game licenses also grew by 8%, while sports licensing remained steady. While Disney has been licensing for over half a century and has over 600 licensees, many professional teams have reduced the number of licenses due to concerns over quality control, the NFL's reduction from 400 to 300 licensees being a case in point. Meanwhile, collegiate licensing continues to expand primarily due to the loyalty of the alumni. In the U.S., over 4000 companies license some form of collegiate merchandise.

In 1980, only $13 billion was generated from all licensed products. In 1994, corporate licensed products alone grossed $13 billion in the U.S. and Canada, while worldwide sales of all licensed goods reached $102 billion.

The number of products that can be licensed is almost endless and can be broadly divided into apparel and hard goods.

Apparel

Items of clothing and associated products are the most popular and biggest selling lines. These range from fashion apparel and coordinates, caps, scarves, T-shirts, sweatshirts to sleepwear, knitwear and raincoats.

Hard goods

These include items such as umbrellas, seat cushions, key rings, cigarette lighters and jewelry. Wines, beers and even restaurant chains are being licensed today. If the licensing organization is not a household name with credibility, the look or appeal of the graphic is important. Some little known college teams in the United States enjoy good licensing revenues principally due to the excitement generated by their logo. The logo should:

- Convey a clear image.
- Have meaning and direction.
- Have great appeal as a graphic.

There are several categories in licensing

- Hot Property. Applies to a fad or a once-only, irregular or unique event.
- Stable Property. Likely to be around for a long time, this category applies to most sports teams and established brand names.
- Indirect Property. If the entity is associated with or is involved in the same endeavor as a current hot property, the opportunity exists to spin off that popularity.
- Personalities. People identify with stars making personalities excellent licensing properties.

To successfully establish your brand for licensing, it is advisable to appoint an agent who will obtain the licensees. Licensees are companies that sell the involvement to third parties, for example, companies who will place logos on merchandise for retail sale to enhance the appeal of the item. This occurs in two ways, through specific appeal to supporters of the property and

This excellent logo for an apparel line for women golfers says it all.

the attraction an exciting design will have to the public at large. Many companies will place a logo, slogan or a sport's star's autograph on a merchandise item to increase its marketability or as part of a promotional campaign.

The principal requirements of a licensee from the licensor's viewpoint are stability, good quality, well designed merchandise and most importantly, good relationships with retailers having excellent distribution. The greater the distribution, the more access the community has to the product and therefore the greater its potential sales.

The Benefits of Merchandising

Merchandising has often been referred to as the greatest marketing tool available to any organization. Not only can merchandising generate extensive exposure and promotion in otherwise unobtainable areas, it emphasizes that the property is important and is supported by the public at large. In addition, merchandising can generate substantial income.

As an indication of the multitude of merchandising applications, major league teams offer up to 250 different licensed items with a further 150 available through retail outlets and catalogs. At the 1994 Super Bowl, over 300,000 merchandise items were sold, generating over $18 million in revenue.

While sport properties are frequently the most visible, corporations are utilizing merchandising more every day. For example, of the literally billions of t-shirts sold each year, few do not carry a logo or message. Harley Davidson have licensed a chain of theme restaurants along the lines of the Hard Rock Cafe and designers such as Pierre Cardin and Gucci have licensed a complete range of products, not only related to fashion.

Corporations need to be cognizant of the fact that the expansion of a brand into a range of `non core business' items can confuse the public and in fact weaken the core brand.

Harley Davidson was recently recognized by the Licensing Industry Merchandisers Association for its brand extension achievements. The merchandise and services licensed by Harley enable everyone to embrace the `culture' without actually owning a Harley Davidson motor bike.

The main reason why an organization licenses its products are;

- To generate income.

- To maintain the allegiance of current consumers.

"Merchandising has often been referred to as the greatest marketing tool available."

"Expansion of a brand into a range of `non core business' items can weaken the core brand."

- To recruit new consumers.

- To generally increase exposure and publicity.

- To provide new, unique opportunities for advertising/promotion.

The main reasons why manufacturers utilize licensing are;

- To increase brand image awareness and front-of-mind recall.

- To provide new and unique opportunities for advertising and promotion

- To be able to offer for sale a product under license which is usually exclusive to that manufacturer, This exclusivity increases potential sales volume.

- A small company can apply creativity to a different license(s) each year rather than having to improve or change the base product.

Prior to entering into an agreement, the potential licensee should always look at who is licensing the property and their track record. Also find out who holds the master license. If it is a major chain, fast food group or beverage, this increases the chance of success as their advertising and promotion power will assist to drive consumer demand.

With an international event such as the Olympic Games, or a project such as the Special Olympics, many corporations license the symbols to achieve a corporate positioning, an image of corporate responsibility or to benefit from the patriotism engendered.

Until recent times, merchandise was produced primarily for children in lower socio-economic groups and distributed through discount or major retail outlets and at the event. Now we have the advent of the up-market boutiques and the authentic teamwear that carries a premium price tag.

This diversification has led to merchandise being defined into several specific market segments.

In order of price and quality, these are;

- Arena and souvenir concession ($1-$20).

- Mass market retail and discount stores (from $10).

- Up-market department stores, primarily in special "sports departments" ($25-$60).

- `Boutique Stores' ($25-$100+).

The fastest growth is in the highly profitable up-market boutique areas which attract buyers with high disposable income.

Major League Baseball Properties, the licensing arm of baseball in the United States, opened its own nationwide chain of retail stores in 1988, selling licensed MLB products and other sports lines. The merchandise includes top-end clothing and an exclusive line of collectibles, apparel and equipment actually used in games.

The power of brand names to sell products can be seen in Las Vegas where the casinos all sell a wide variety of self branded merchandise with some items costing thousands of dollars.

Overall, merchandising is likely to experience considerable real growth over the next decade, as it becomes an increasingly important component of the marketing, brand awareness mix and an increasingly important profit center. The opportunity exists for all corporations, sports bodies and organizations, whether large or small, to capitalize on this growth.

Terminology Used in Licensing:

Irrespective of whether the marketer determines to license their own merchandise or to utilize the services of a specialist, it is essential to understand the industry terminology. The most commonly used terms are:

Licensing

The owner of the copyright on the logo or slogan, generally through an agent, will grant a license to another company, usually a manufacturer, to reproduce the logo or slogan on, or in conjunction with, the manufacturer's product. Personalities can also be licensed. The majority, whose fame may be short lived, are regarded as HOT property. Those with longevity become a STABLE property. For example, Gucci and Jack Nicklaus, who have been leading merchandise properties for well over a decade, are regarded as stable properties.

Licensor

The owner of the copyright on the logo or slogan.

Licensee

The person to whom the license is granted.

Retail

The license is granted to companies who manufacture the product and then market them through retail stores, clubs, direct marketing or on-site retail organizations. For example, a company making car seat covers displaying the Los Angeles Lakers logo sells them to service stations and motor sports retail stores who then sell them to the public. The seat covers displaying the Gucci label sell through up-market department stores.

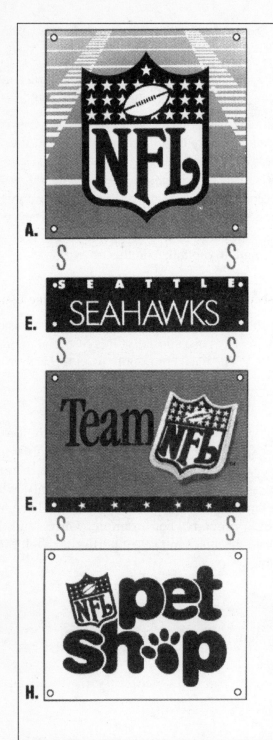

A. NFL Shield

The classic NFL Shield printed over a football field. 30" x 30" printed both sides on a sturdy cardboard.

B. The OLP Seal

The Officially Licensed Product Seal. Three dimensional, pressure formed, foil plaque measures 9" x 16".

C. T-Stand Topper Cards

NFLP's new T-Stand Topper cards are printed with your home team's helmet. Perfect for Quad Racks or T-Stands, these sturdy 5½" X 7" cardboard signs are available in all 28 teams and the NFL shield. (Shipped 5 cards per pack, please specify team.)

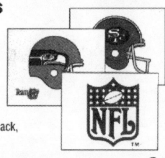

E. NFL Team Shop Sign System

Attractive new signs for 1990 updates last year's NFL Team Shop System. Sturdy cardboard Team NFL Sign (20" x 30") matches your home team's strip sign (10" x 30") to create one 30" x 30" unit. Grommets and S-hooks are enclosed to help you create your own system.

H. Segmented Marketing P.O.P. Pieces

Focus on your specialty business with these colorful Logo Signs. Printed on both sides, these 20" x 30" signs work independently or in conjunction with the Team NFL P.O.P. Made of sturdy cardboard stock and shipped with grommetts and "S" hooks. Logo Signs are available for each of the programs shown below. Specify quantity and logo desired.

Courtesy: NFL Properties

The NFL provides full point of sale support to retailers selling NFL licensed properties. The promotional piece above details some of the elements available to create color, impact, encourage multiple sales and increase dollar per square foot revenue. The NFL shield, Team NFL, Specialty P.O.S. pieces and Home Team Strip signs are supplied with all fittings and "S" hooks. Exciting neon signs in various sizes and NFL carpeting representing the playing field are also available to assist in merchandise promotion.

Promotional

The licensor grants licenses to companies who use the logo or slogan to promote or associate its own product with the licensee's product. Good examples are VISA card's association with the Olympic Games and the fast food chain tie-ins with major movie releases.

Royalty

The royalty varies from a percentage of the wholesale value of every item sold in the case of a retail license, to a flat fee in the case of promotional licenses. It may be a combination of both. With retail licenses, the royalty usually ranges from 5% to 10% of the wholesale price for stable properties and 10% to 15% for hot properties.

The trend is to an increase in royalties, most hot properties now being in the teens. This is secured against a minimum guarantee usually consisting of a non-refundable advance of between 25-60% of the total guaranteed sales in each license period. The typical deal is for two years, the range being from one to five years. If the guaranteed sales in the year of the contract are not achieved, the licensee will pay the shortfall. Guarantees from licenses are very important because;

a) If a licensee guarantees a minimum performance, they will work harder to achieve the sales target.
b) The owner of the property can't live on potential. Guarantees form a minimum base income for that property for the specific period.

In the case of a promotional license, the licensor will assess the value of the license to the licensee in either monetary or exposure/ association terms. This is usually based on a combination of comparable promotions and what the market will bear.

Properties

The term property applies to the actual logo, motif, or slogan protected by trademark or copyright. These include the various logos for sports teams, the Los Angeles Raiders, the West Coast Eagles, the New York Giants, etc.. The Olympic rings, Wimbledon, World Cup and U.S. Open tennis logos are examples of event properties. The symbols for Mercedes Benz, Cartier and Gucci are corporate properties while Superman, Alf, and Mickey Mouse are examples of cartoon properties. Stable or Long Term properties are those who enjoy longevity, principally without change over an extended period of time.

With event licenses, licensors try to sell in.early to ensure they are in a position for the licensees to react quickly to produce merchandise for retailers if the demand occurs.

The Importance of Appointing Licensing Agencies:

While it is not essential to appoint an agency to procure licensees fo a property, this option offers considerable advantages. It is possible to pro cure licensees directly, however, it is a very time consuming exercise. Th on-course committee of the inaugural Australian Formula One Grand Pri of which I was a member, undertook to procure its own licensees and ove a twelve month period obtained in excess of 150 different products carry ing the various Formula One and event logos.

The advantages an agency provides are their expertise and their cor stant ear to the ground and knowledge of who is doing what. They know the best manufacturers for each type of product, the range of product available, the companies with the best distribution, financial stability an reliability. The knowledge of distribution capability is extremely impo tant. Product categories of a licensed product may be sold to chain and di count stores, specialty or departmental, in addition to hardware, spor stores, toy and gift shops. Promotional licensing rights may be bought b fast food chains, soft drink or snack food manufacturers, in fact, they ma be utilized for an advertising campaign for any kind of product. A spe cialist is required to determine which manufacturer has good creativ effective distribution into the appropriate sales outlets and desirable loca tion. Some T-shirts companies, for example, only sell through discoun stores, others through specialty and department stores. The licensor als enjoys the benefit of the promotion done by agencies to promote the pro ucts they have under license.

In the majority of cases, income from licensing is dependent on pay ment per item sold and the agent is skilled in monitoring actual sales an ensuring that all sales are credited. The agent is also aware of the merchar dise selling in the marketplace, the current trends and the treatment tha can be affected to a property to make it more commercial.

To achieve the best results with most licensed properties, a total licens ing concept should be sold to a retailer. An individual product licensee car not do this as effectively as a licensing agent. The agent is seen to be sellin the concept while the licensee is seen to be selling only their produc Licensed products offered in a concept shop frequently enjoy better sale than a T-shirt in the clothing department, or caps in the hat departmen This knowledge of which manufacturer has 'access', makes an agent ver valuable. Licensing consultants usually work on a retainer and a sma commission.

Final Responsibility

The final approval on all designs, or advertising/promotion trea ments utilized by various licensees and the type of products that ar licensed remains with the licensor. The agent, unless given specifi approval, is always the licensee's servant. The product should be checke at every stage of production. The rough design, finished art, prototype an then the final product must be approved prior to mass manufacture. I addition, all packaging must be approved to ensure it reflects the produ

> **"To achieve the best results a total licensing concept should be sold to a retailer."**

> **"The agent, unless given specific approval, is always the licensee's servant."**

image as well as promoting the name or property and achieving the aims which initiated the involvement.

Follow Through

To maximize the endeavors of the agent or licensee, and support the retailer's sales effort, the following methods can be used:

- Point of sale material. The production of striking posters, cut-outs or mobiles for display in the retail outlets.
- Produce photographs that include the merchandise to generate publicity.
- Appearance by star athletes, full size characters or 'props' that represent the product being licensed, e.g. placement of a race car or appearances by team members in retail outlets.
- A wide range of promotions and consumer competitions can be held which focus on the products. The most popular types of promotions are in-pack or on-pack.
- Telephone marketing.
- Cross promotion with the manufacturers and a third party. For example, a Washington Redskins pen that also promotes the local Ford dealer.

Protect the License

The key to protecting against trademark infringements is diligent observation of the market place to identify any "bootleg" product. Once identified, it is simple to obtain a court order preventing the manufacturers or seller from offering the product and allowing confiscation of the offending materials. One of my favorites is the advertisement that was run in trade publications by MCA/Universal to discourage "bootlegging" of Jurassic Park merchandise.

The Steven Spielberg movie, Jurassic Park, was one of the great licensing success stories in history. The notices run in trade magazines left no doubt that they were going to protect their licensees.

Allocate Licenses Carefully

The principal requirements of a licensee from the licensor's viewpoint are stability, excellent creativity, good quality, well designed merchandise and most importantly, good relationships with retailers/distributors with excellent market penetration and marketing support. The greater the distribution, the more access the community has to the product and therefore the greater the potential sales.

The licensor is also concerned that if the product really takes off, the licensee has the infrastructure and the financial ability to be able to meet the demand. Also, most leagues today share revenues between teams and licensees need to create designs and produce product not just for one team but for every team in the league. This increases the licensors concern regarding capability to produce.

Most properties can be used in a variety of ways and its is not uncommon to have several licensees manufacturing their own range of T-shirts, sweat shirts or jackets incorporating a particular organization's property yet each being completely different. To achieve this successfully, the parameters of individual licensees must be extremely well defined.

Each manufacturer in turn will have a selection of styles and colors to ensure greater appeal to a wider variety of customers. If the licensee is contracted for more than one year it is often a condition of the license that the styles must be redesigned in subsequent years. Frequently, licensees will produce different item designs for various retail chains in order to provide "exclusives."

Summary

Like direct mail and sales promotion, licensing is another sales tool which when it adds value to the product, is highly effective. For a successful result, the licensor must be able to explain how a licensing program benefits the manufacturer, retailer and consumer. While using the goodwill and accumulated value of an established property can be beneficial in selling a product, including a character or celebrity it will not necessarily guarantee millions of items sold. There is a lot of licensed product out there with little value to the consumer.

Licensors need to select product lines carefully as a few poor products could convert a success into a perceived failure. For corporate brand extension licensing, the same situation applies.

Volume is not necessarily the answer to successful licensing… quality is!

"Volume is not necessarily the answer to successful licensing… quality is!"

Chapter **10** # Endorsements

Many celebrities, successful businessmen and athletes reflect the positive values that we as individuals and as a community respect and seek to emulate: hard work, desire, concentration, intensity, physical fitness, good health, respect and success.

Consequently, some of the largest advertising deals involve staggering sums of money for celebrities to endorse almost every conceivable type of product.

While it may initially appear that only the top athletes or celebrities endorse products, or are utilized in merchandising, there are innumerable opportunities in this growing field for a host of respected public figures. However, the combination of the right personality and the right product is crucial to endorsement success.

During the period Pepsi-Cola sponsored Michael Jackson's concert tours for $20 million, Pepsi claims to have picked up two market share points on Coca-Cola...worth $500 million per point in annual sales.

Ex-Chicago Bears' football star Walter Payton sold Wheaties to Americans, Ray Charles won't share his Pepsi, Greg Norman tells us Swan Beer is better, Chris Evert is always nice to be near with Rexona Deodorant, the Mean Machine Gold Medal swim team live on Buttercup Bread and marathon champion Robert de Castella lept for Toyota.

Before a corporation decides to utilize a personality as an endorser, they must know that the individual will be credible to the public with the product they are endorsing. The public would not accept 310 pound N.F.L.

star William "the Refrigerator" Perry endorsing Weight Watchers. You could imagine him eating a dozen hamburgers and french fries every day but not a low calorie, lowfat, small portion dinner.

Personalities as endorsers offer great opportunities for brand awareness and recall but potentially offer great dangers as well.

Unless the personality is renowned for clean living, it is very dangerous for a corporation to closely associate a long term campaign with one presenter. The corporation runs the risk of the talent going to jail, going bankrupt or becoming involved in behavior that may damage the image of their product.

Tying in a product with a celebrity does not guarantee instant success. The 1993 study by the Athletics Footwear Association in America showed only 10% of people would buy a product because of a celebrity endorsement, the least important of 10 motivations to purchase.

If the presenter is better known than the product, the public remembers the presenter rather than the product. When the balance between presenter and product is equitable, endorsements are hard to beat. Health cereal Nutri-Grain, endorsed by iron man Grant Kenny, enjoyed an increase of over 100% in its share of the Australian breakfast cereal market. Olympic Gold medalist swimmer Lisa Curry's campaign for Uncle Toby's Muesli Bars resulted in a 300% increase in that product's sales.

The key ingredients for any successful campaign using presenters are consistency and continuity.

The international campaign for Energizer batteries featuring former football personality Mark Jackson had very high impact, creating immediate attention, controversy and brand awareness. The public either loved or hated Jackson but everyone noticed the advertisements. The campaign began in Australia and was extended to the United States where, although being a total unknown, he signed a reported $3 million contract to promote Eveready. Risky? In 1971 Fila signed a new young tennis prospect named Bjorn Borg. Certainly it is a risk, but it is a very well calculated one.

It is also very important for the endorser to choose the products they endorse very carefully. In 1981, singer Pat Boone was the first endorser to be ordered to pay refunds to dissatisfied users of an acne medication he endorsed. In 1989, actor Lloyd Bridges agreed to take some financial responsibility for a commercial in which he endorsed a corporation that went out of business. In this case, Bridges was sued by investors in the corporation. A similar situation involved actor George Hamilton. As a result, it is essential for athletes and their agents to be diligent in assessing the merits of their endorsements and to demand final approval on the scripts.

If a personality goes astray, so does the effectiveness of the advertising campaign. Immediately after Pepsi launched the Mike Tyson campaign, a host of magazine articles alleged Tyson to be a wife beater. The California Egg Commission cancelled its endorsement agreement with Oakland Athletic star Jose Canseco when he was arrested for allegedly carrying a loaded semi automatic pistol in his car. These indiscretions are extremely difficult to anticipate.

"Personalities as endorser's offer great opportunities but potentially offer great dangers as well."

"If a personality goes astray, so does the effectiveness of the advertising campaign."

The Guidelines To Follow:

Experience shows that presenters frequently score high on recall but low on effectiveness to sell product. To achieve both, corporations must follow several guidelines:

- Presenter must be relevant to the product.
- Select the talent carefully.
- Maintain the talent/product balance.
- Don't use an overexposed personality.
- Spread the risk.
- Keep the message relevant.

1. **The Presenter Must Be Relevant To The Product**
    The personality must "fit" the product, because without relevance, there will be a credibility gap that will adversely affect product sales. If the product requires integrity and authority, a highly respected business leader may portray those qualities. A colorful, entertaining product requires a flamboyant, effervescent personality, while a health item demands a well-proportioned, healthy-looking athlete. For example, the use of New York Yankee Dave Winfield in advertisements for a children's toothbrush was an excellent choice as American children knew Winfield and could emulate his actions, therefore encouraging the use of the particular toothbrush. Matching the athlete with products used in their sport, such as John Daly with a new golf club, Andre Agassi and a tennis racquet or Michael Schumacher with a new brand of tire is certainly a major credibility advantage for the products. The public must believe that the personality would use the product for the endorsement to be effective.

2. **Select The Personality Very Carefully**
    People are fallible, and because of high incomes, public adulation and constant pressure, celebrities are often more so than most. Before the presenter is selected, their backgrounds should be checked to find any potentially negative character flaws. Do they drink too much? Could they be a public embarrassment or hit the headlines on a drunk driving charge? Do they have a history of violence on the field? Are there stories of infidelity? If the answer to such questions could be yes, the personality should not be used. Avoid using anyone who could make the headlines in a manner that could damage the product.

3. **Don't Use An Overexposed Personality**
    Presenters will overshadow the product message if they are already widely known for endorsing a range of other products and this will damage the value of the endorsement. The personality merely becomes a presenter and not a "true believer" in the product.

"The personality must "fit" the product, because without relevance, there will be a credibility gap that will adversely affect product sales."

"People are fallible, celebrities more so than most."

4. **Maintaining The Balance Between Talent And Product**
    The presenter should be utilized sufficiently to endorse the product without interfering with the message that highlights the reasons to buy the product. The presenter must not take the limelight away from the product.

5. **Spread The Risk**
    If the advertising budget allows for more than one celebrity, it dilutes the impression of any one personality "owning" the product. At the same time it may broaden the product's appeal and create the impression on the consumer that the product is widely used by personalities. Like any high profile personality, individual celebrities are both liked and dislike by different sections of the community. By spreading the appeal, the product becomes associated with the whole community.

6. **Keep The Message Relevant**
    The script must be in keeping with the presenters normal speech and should not appear artificial. If it sounds out of character the endorser and the product become non- believable. A major advantage of sports personalities is they usually relate very well to the average person. This communication level must be maintained in the advertisement.

Athletes and entertainers are effective and successful presenters for many products because of the enormous respect they command from the community. The advertising industry boasts many triumphs and few failures and if the basic rules set out above are followed, this trend should continue.

However, in my view, there may also be an increased use of "manufactured" endorsers as a result of the failure of some celebrity campaigns and the risks associated with 'stars'.

With the increase in social awareness and responsibility in the community, the perception of who is a "hero" may also be changing. Landscapes On-Line research in 1995 produced a survey that showed that to the upscale consumer, a hero is someone, male or female, who helps human kind (63%), while 34% considered someone who surmounts difficult hurdles as a hero. Only 3% looked up to a person who broke a record and 94% considered it inconsequential. For example, while Mother Teresa (91%), Michelangelo (84%) and Greg Louganis (66%), Olympic Gold medalist who admitted to being homosexual, rated well, Babe Ruth, Michael Jordan and Patrick Ewing all rated below 20%.

The public, strange as it may initially appear, find invented characters such as Joe Isuzu for Isuzu Motors, Jim Bodette for Motel 6, Ed and Frank for Bartles and James and even Bud Light's Spuds MacKenzie more credible than celebrities and athletes. A study carried out by Video Storyboard Tests "Commercial Break" revealed only 17% of the public approved of celebrity/athlete endorsements. Moreover, 52% said celebrities/athletes lack credibility, 64% believe they are only in it for the money and 37% don't believe they actually use the product.

If this public credibility gap continues, corporations will become increasingly selective with celebrity endorsers.

> "Individual celebrities are both liked and disliked by different sections of the community."

> "The public find invented characters more credible than celebrities and athletes."

Chapter 11   Hospitality

"Corporate hospitality is a form of professional foreplay."

"Corporate hospitality is a form of professional foreplay." This quote sums up the benefits of hospitality as a marketing tool.

One of the most important forms of corporate involvement in events today is the hospitality opportunities associated with these events. From the corporate viewpoint, hospitality is not new. It is derived from the business lunch and takes place during a day at an event.

Events utilizing hospitality are the most involving and intimate of all communication forms. They allow products, services and enthusiastic personnel to spend quality time with customers or potential customers in a relaxed situation. Events may allow an hour, a day or a week away from the telephones, engaging in one-on-one communication. This is compared with 30 seconds on a broadcast medium or 15 minutes on a sales call.

This development of a personal relationship and increased understanding between the corporation and its client will enable better communication after the event and an increased sales growth potential. Further, socializing engenders goodwill, which in turn relates almost to an obligation for the person receiving the hospitality to reciprocate through the business connection.

For example, motor oil manufacturer STP uses NASCAR and Indy racing as its sports marketing vehicle. Public relations director Harvey Duck says, *"Auto racing is a hell of a medium to entertain your customers. You can't sell one can of STP if it's not on the shelf. To get it there you wine and dine the buyer."*

For event organizations, hospitality represents a major growth area in income in return for a relatively small financial outlay.

Fan support is no longer the principal factor in the success of sport franchises. Gate receipts and media revenues are now competing with stadium advertising, concession agreements and luxury boxes for importance.

In 1995, two NFL teams, the Raiders and Rams, left the second largest television market in the world (Los Angeles) for `city' incentives and an increase in the number of luxury boxes. The Raiders returned to Oakland because of an increase in the number of boxes from 58 to 175 at the Oakland Coliseum.

A luxury box is not an inexpensive investment. Suites at many stadiums can cost up to $250,000 per year. I once read a wonderful quote that said *"At Madison Square Garden, boxes offer a view of the action that reduces seven foot tall basketball players to ants in short pants".*

Corporate hospitality is a form of professional foreplay."

They allow enthusiastic personnel to spend quality time with customers or potential customers in a relaxed situation."

At the United Center in Chicago, the home of the Bulls and th
Blackhawks, the 216 suites sell for between $55,000 to $175,000 each pe
year and offset the cost ($175 million) the teams contributed to construc
ing the facility.

As an added bonus, hospitality opportunities are more acceptable an
easier to justify to many corporations than traditional sponsorships. The
can be individually priced at an affordable level most companies can relat
to in sales-cost terms. They also provide a high margin of profit to the eve
organization. The demand for premium facilities, providing comfort, pr
vacy and excellent viewing is extremely strong and this demand will co
tinue to increase as more corporations utilize the benefits of hospitality a
a way to partially, but effectively, offset high media costs and increasing
fragmented audiences.

Hospitality opportunities are viewed in importance by corporatio
to an extent that almost without exception, the premium packages are th
first to sell out.

Hospitality as a Corporate Marketing Tool:

When doing business, the main priority is to maintain the client an
maximize the volume of business obtained. For this to happen, a relationshi
based on respect and trust needs to be established between the corporatio
and its customer. There is a high cost involved in "cold calling," that i
approaching a potential client that is not known, or is not known well, i
order to sell a product or service. More importantly, the opportunity t
develop a relationship is minimal. *Marketing Week* estimates that in mo
businesses selling a premium product, the cost of making a cold call is in th
order of $250-$300 with absolutely no guarantee of success. When cold cal
ing, it is also difficult to get to the person who makes the decisions. By co
trast, the decision maker will usually attend a high profile event. Hospitali
provides not only a qualified call but affords the host considerable time t
make an effective impression under much more favorable conditions tha
the pressures created by a business office environment. Although not ine
pensive, corporate hospitality is generally less expensive and significant
more effective than other means of getting to know a client.

The hosting of a hospitality facility at an event elevates a corpor
tion's image and if the host corporation is seen to be obtaining tickets tha
are normally difficult, or better still impossible to get, the company's pre
tige in the eyes of the guests will be even further enhanced. Hospitalit
facilities at events are patronized by business leaders from a range c
industries providing the opportunity to meet socially with importar
executives associated with other corporate groups.

Hospitality can also be an effective technique in motivating a corpor
tion's own sales force. The corporation's staff will give up their time abov
and beyond the call of duty in order to attend an event. Attendance at co
porate hospitality facilities, particularly those at exclusive events or ove
seas, represents an attractive incentive for increased performance.

"The decision maker will usually attend a high profile event."

"An effective technique in motivating a corporation's own sales force."

Different corporations have varying hospitality needs. The Dow Corporation undertook sponsorship of the World Series Open Tennis Championship in Washington D.C. to upgrade its public image, entertain clients and improve relations with U.S. politicians. As a result, the corporation believes that members of the government administration now see Dow as "more cooperative people."

Dow entertained 175 clients and politicians each day in the hospitality tent and at other functions, conducted a business seminar and dinner for 125 customers at the tournament. In addition Dow entertained over 400 people at the Dow banquet after the Pro-Am event.

Hospitality Facilities are in High Demand...

The Alabama International Speedway in Tulladega, Atlanta has a 24 Marquee Hospitality Village as an addendum to the VIP boxes that have been sold out for many years. This hospitality village also has a waiting list with companies such as Miller Brewing, General Foods, Budweiser, and Chevrolet fully utilizing the facilities offered. The designer tents are attractively presented, each having a patio area enclosed by a picket fence. Despite being less permanent, the Hospitality Village is as popular as the VIP suites because corporations can entertain up to 100 people with full catering, entertainment and security at any time, in contrast to only 24 people who can enjoy the VIP box.

"Different corporations have varying hospitality needs."

Courtesy: Alabama International Speedway

The Hospitality Village provides 100 guest passes, entertainment, closed circuit television, reserved parking, food and liquor facilities.

Summary

Hospitality is an inexpensive method of creating client goodwill and sales, being especially effective in stimulating repeat business. In 1995, the cost of entertaining a guest at the Epsom Derby in England was $200.00 $250.00 at the American Open Golf tournament, and $500.00 a Wimbledon. However, prior to deciding to host clients or potential client at an event, it is important to determine whether the same or better resul could be obtained by taking a client out for lunch on a one-to-one basis, o even providing a gift or incentive. This is a decision that can only be deter mined by the individual company.

The Corporate Hospitality Check List:

Offering corporate hospitality at an event to an established or potentia client can be one of the most effective means of obtaining repeat business and generating new orders. However, unless carefully planned, corporate hospi tality can be an embarrassment that may destroy those opportunities. It i important to have a check list to guarantee a successful event.

Determine the Suitability of the Event

Frequently, providing hospitality to clients at smaller events offer significant advantages over the larger, exclusive events. Small events offe increased opportunity to extend the corporation's presence through spon sorship, signage, product use by the participants and advertisements ir the program. This additional exposure creates a more favorable impres sion on the corporation's guests. It is also important to investigate oppor tunities to extend the involvement to prevent ambushing by a competitor

The more prestigious events are usually considerably more expen sive, offer less opportunities and afford comparison with the hospitality facilities offered by other corporations.

Check the Suppliers Credentials

It is important to check the credentials of the company providing the hospitality facilities. There is an increasing number of organizations pro moting themselves as hospitality companies who have a less than satis factory performance record. Check whether the company is operating offi cially and establish the source of the event tickets.

Confirm the Seat Location

Unofficial companies often offer hospitality packages to exclusive events with tickets that are not in prime positions. This may result ir either paying too much for the overall package or worse, considerabl embarrassment if the tickets either fail to materialize, have impeded vision or are in the back row.

> "Corporate hospitality can be an embarrassment that may destroy opportunities."

Seat the Guests Together

Ensure the guests will be sitting together. Frequently, hospitality packages have guest seating scattered throughout a particular area.

Extend the Corporate Image

Since you are going to the expense of creating a good image you should ensure you extend your corporate image. The small details are very important when considering client hospitality. The corporate logo and theme, if one has been developed for the occasion, should be extended from the initial invitation to the marquee table, welcome documents, event itinerary and other possible applications. These details reinforce to the client the positive image of their host, their attention to detail, corporate pride and stature. The corporation's name on the outside of the hospitality area also creates a favorable impression with others attending the event.

"The small details are very important."

Check the Involvement of Competitors

It is important to check the involvement of competitors prior to arranging hospitality at an event. If competitors have a sponsorship position, signage, or are the official product suppliers, this may have a detrimental effect on the image of the host.

Ensure the Event and Guests are Compatible

When selecting an event, don't let your own preferences cloud your judgement. Ensure the event and guests are compatible. Many corporations make the mistake of allowing their own event preferences to over-ride what their guests may enjoy. Prior to inviting a client to an event, discreet enquires should be made to ensure the client and their spouse or partners are likely to enjoy the activity. It is also important that people who have been allocated to sit together at a table are compatible. Always have one of the host corporation's personnel at each table.

"Don't let your own preferences cloud your judgement."

Prioritize the Guest List

Many events are spread over several days and some days are more important than others. The invitation list should be graded to ensure the most important clients are invited to the premier days.

Be Specific with Hospitality Benefits

It is important to know exactly what the hospitality package includes.

- Does it include drinks? Is there an open bar throughout the day or do drinks have to paid for? The latter situation may be embarrassing to guests and alternative arrangements should be made.
- Are the event programs supplied? If so, guests should be advised in order that they do not buy one when they arrive at the entrance gate.

Confirm Any Special Dietary Requirements

There are several things you should do to ensure the maximum impact on your guests. The first is to confirm any special dietary requirements. Many people have particular dietary requirements and this should be determined when issuing the invitation so arrangements can be made with the caterer.

Check the Location of the Facilities

It is essential to know exactly where the hospitality facilities are located. Near the venue may mean a substantial walk or even being transported to the actual event. The ideal location is in the midst of the action, providing clients with a base for the day and a point to which they can easily return, for example, in the case of rain.

Communicate the Specific Arrangements

"The client needs to be confident of the arrangements or is unlikely to arrive."

When advising your clients of their invitation be sure to communicate the specific arrangements. The client needs to be confident of the details or is unlikely to arrive. This includes the formality of the invitation, the distribution of tickets, a detailed itinerary, arrival and finishing time, arrangements for parking and establishing a dress code to save the guest from uncertainty or embarrassment. Specify clearly whether the invitation is for one or two guests. It is also frequently important for guests to be contactable, so details of a contact phone number and the location is often valuable information.

Prevent Confusion

If the hospitality arrangements are not private but include a luncheon in a VIP area being utilized by a number of corporations, it is essential your guests know where they are sitting and with whom.

Don't Drink and Drive

"Provide transport for hospitality guests at events where any significant quantity of alcohol is likely to be consumed."

It is recommended to provide transport for hospitality guests at events where any significant quantity of alcohol is likely to be consumed. This avoids the possible consequences of drinking and driving.

Summary

All of this can be facilitated by being a good host. Representatives of the host corporation must be at the event, comfortable and relaxed prior to the arrival of any guests.

Most important of all, utilize the quality time. It is imperative that the host's representatives do not browbeat a client with heavy business discussions but are sociable and able to talk quietly in a relaxed manner in pleasant surroundings. To enable dialogue to be maintained, the hospitality site should be close to the event action.

Observance of these few pointers will ensure that corporate hospitality is one of the most successful marketing techniques available in developing client relationships.

12 Sponsorship

Without corporate sponsorship, the majority of sports teams and events would not exist as we know them today. However, in the past, the lack of a truly professional approach has prevented the majority of sponsors from maximising their investment. The result is corporate disillusion, making sponsorships more difficult to obtain.

"The American approach to marketing events has been a Rambo approach, you take what's hot, and what you end up with is a laundry list of sponsors jumping into one big event, and no sponsor able to figure out a way to justify his money"...Robert E. Hope, executive vice president, world wide marketing at Burson-Marsteller.

300% Growth in 8 Years

Despite this disillusion, the growth in both the number of entities seeking sponsorships and corporations providing sponsorships has increased considerably in recent years. Corporations are demanding a return on their investment and sport and event organizations not fulfilling that return are destined for oblivion.

More than 5,000 U.S. companies in 1995 spent US $4.7 billion sponsoring sport and events, an increase of 300% in eight years, says *IEG Sponsorship Report*. This growth pattern is reflected across the world. Moreover, growth in event sponsorship over the next five years is estimated to exceed 100%.

Why Sponsorship is Effective

Numerous reasons motivate companies to sponsor events and their involvement varies considerably dependent upon the company's products, its image, budget considerations and its overall marketing and advertising policies. In recent years, several factors have contributed to the growth in event sponsorship.

1. The proliferation of media vehicles has caused reduced audiences and higher CPM (cost per thousand impacts).
2. The consumer market has become more highly segmented with dual incomes, single parents, the "gray power" growth and so on.
3. Media advertising cost has increased at three times the consumer price index since the early 1980's.

4.   Rapid increase in the volume of advertisements, advertorial content infomercials and 15 second television advertisements, all contributing to message clutter.

5.   Profusion of brands, increased competition and decreased consume loyalty. Product life cycles are shrinking at an increasing rate.

6.   Shift in importance from the consumer to the retailer/trade for shel space, prime location and promotion.

These influences have caused corporations to seek alternative com munication vehicles.

The Public is Sportsminded

The widely reported and quoted Miller Brewing study illustrates the public's affinity with sports and events. Some findings of the study:

- 74% of the public watch sports on television at least once a week.
- 70% watch, read or discuss sport or sports news at least once a day.
- 46% of the public participates in at least one athletic activity every day or almost every day.
- 74% believe that athletes make good role models for children.
- 59% believe athletes make the best role models.
- 19% of the public are characterized as "avid sports fans."
- 66% of teenagers are classified as "avid sports participants."
- 75% of parents encourage their children to participate in sports.
- 85% of parents watch their children compete in sports.

In The United States The Public Appreciates Sponsorship

The research firm McKeon and Associates tracks audience recognition of, and attitudes to, sponsors. In 1993, they conducted this research at the Chicago Gospel Festival and the Chicago Blues Festival. The results were:

- A positive image of the sponsors - Blues Festival   94.4%
                                     - Gospel Festival   95.4%

- Improves likelihood of buying sponsors product
                                     - Blues Festival   73.0%
                                     - Gospel Festival   82.2%

More importantly,   43.5% could identify the Blues Festival majo: sponsor and 63% identified the Gospel Festival sponsor. One month later 70.5% could still name at least one of the corporate sponsors.

In these surveys, the statistics held across age and earnings categories with strength of product loyalty increasing slightly with income levels.

The findings demonstrate that effectively implemented event sponsorship provides companies with a lifestyle bonding and a strong recall factor, both of which are essential in developing brand loyalty. The results will vary depending on the nature of the event and the demographics of its audience but from all of the surveys I have seen the pattern is a similar one.

The Australian Public's Attitude

Research into the public attitude to sponsorship carried out in Australia in 1993 by Brian Sweeney and Associates provided significantly different results to the U.S. Studies.

	Agree	Disagree	Neutral
• Sponsorship is a good idea	97%	1%	2%
• Too much money is spent on sponsorship	18%	11%	71%
• Without sponsors, sports would be worse off	91%	3%	6%
• There is far too much sponsorship	15%	5%	80%
• I hardly notice who sponsors what	65%	8%	28%
• They only do it for their own benefit	62%	8%	30%
• I prefer to buy sponsors products	27%	16%	57%

Having been associated with event marketing at a major event level in both the United States and Australia for many years, the Australian public's attitude is to a large degree a measure of corporate ineptitude with respect to event marketing. It reflects poor communication of the corporations 'synergy' with the events supporters and poor communication of their association with the event.

United Kingdom Results

The 1993 results of Questel's annual qualitative survey of 12,000 people 14 years and older produced the following key findings;

- Sponsorship is seen as a subtle, less expensive form of advertising.
- There is not any major public resistance or skepticism towards sponsorship The public believes sponsors help keep ticket prices down, maintain less popular events and ensure variety and choice in sport and the arts.

Sponsorship provides companies with a lifestyle bonding and a strong recall factor, both of which are essential in developing brand loyalty."

The Australian public's attitude is to a large degree a measure of corporate ineptitude."

- Consumers expect obvious links between the sponsor and the even They expect relevance, compatibility and a visible partnership

- Active disapproval or even suspicion of sponsorship is rare, and in fa the reverse is true with a high level of goodwill flowing to consumers.

Swedish Results

Swedish based Clark Marketing examined sponsorship effectivenes in that country and obtained a very positive result. In a representativ example, the major sponsor of an event recorded a 40% awareness wit fans of the sport and 18% of them preferred the sponsor to its competitor Of those not interested in the sport, 29% had an awareness of the sponso ship and only 10% preferred the sponsor to its competitors. Very impo tantly, 22% of the sports fans had seen the sponsors non-sponsorshi themed ads compared to 9% of those indifferent to the sport.

Summary

One of the key findings of these surveys is that the public expects a syr ergy to be established between the event and the sponsor. Sponsorship alor will not achieve the desired results. For example, *Sponsor Watch*, a divisio of DDB Needham Worldwide in Chicago, tracked 37 1992 Olympic sponso and 22 created no connection between consumers and the Olympics.

The Objectives of Event Sponsorship:

"The public expects a synergy to be established between the event and the sponsor."

Sponsors utilize event marketing to:

1. Create brand awareness, ideal for product introduction.
2. Reposition brand to alter target market.
3. Revitalize brand to recover lost positioning.
4. Enhance brand by providing vitality through event association.
5. Reinforce brand positioning to current users.
6. Sample product to potential trade or consumers.
7. Improve corporate image to public by event association.
8. Match competitor's involvement more easily and less expensively than in mass media communication.
9. Improve customer relationships through hospitality.
10. Provide opportunity for customer/retailer/trade promotions.
11. Create product credibility by lifestyle or "good image" association.
12. Obtain cost efficient alternative exposure.

The Most Common Reasons Marketers Sponsor Events

Advertising Age in the United States published the following results a survey undertaken to determine the most common reasons markete sponsor events;

1. Increase awareness of company or product name.
2. Identification with a particular lifestyle.
3. Differentiate product from competitors.
4. Enhance commitment to community or ethnic group.
5. Entertain key clients; business-to-business marketing.
6. Merchandising opportunities.
7. Shape or reinforce the public's perception of a product's attributes.
8. Impact the bottom line.

Rick May, Manager of Sports Marketing for Valvoline, whose investment in event marketing began in 1984 and has subsequently grown each year, said, *We're achieving 3 goals: to sell product, increase brand awareness and enhance our relationship with customers and suppliers."*

In a survey we conducted in 1993, corporations were asked to list the importance of various factors when evaluating an event marketing vehicle. The overall percentage attributed to the major considerations were:

- audience size, demographics   87%
- geographic market covered   78%
- track record, credibility   62%
- event positioning, vitality   54%

Event sponsorship creates cost efficient opportunities for lifestyle identification, entertainment for customers, product differentiation and provides an alternative, less expensive communication vehicle.

Sponsorships create a bond between the event and the sponsor's message and enhance that message. Studies conducted by Pritchard Marketing Inc. in 1992 in the United States found that:

- 67% of respondents would buy a product because of the sponsorship (if all else was relatively equal).

- 61% had a more positive view of the company because of the sponsorship.

Events Provide Additional Benefits

A television commercial provides no additional exposure beyond the on-air time, yet correctly constructed sponsorships gain widespread exposure for the sponsor through the events, associated promotions and from the extensive news, human interest and magazine-style stories on participants, results and associated activities.

A significant benefit of event involvement to a corporation is that the public watches and relates in a relaxed and receptive way, in contrast to the resistance presented by the obvious sell of conventional advertising. This increases the effective communication of the sponsor's message.

"Sponsorships create a bond between the event and the sponsor's message and enhance that message."

Sponsorship is a Specific Purpose Investment

Most companies have a wide range of options to obtain exposure fo their products. Beyond advertising, the majority of companies receiv large numbers of sponsorship requests.

The needs of companies vary considerably and every sponsor ha differing requirements for their sponsorship as described earlier. Some ar image enhancement, some altruistic. It may be a combination of many dif ferent motives. Unless the proposal is in line with a company's corporate marketing philosophy and strategy it will not get past first base.

Effective event marketing is not only putting the corporate name or athlete jerseys or signs on stadium walls. It is specialized marketing which includes advertising, promotions, public relations, merchandise, point-of- sale in-store promotions, product give-aways and product tie-in competitions.

Is all Sponsorship Effective?:

Once the event vehicle is determined, there are other factors to be taker into account.

The *IEG Sponsorship Report* released the findings of a 1993 survey o sports enthusiasts by the Roper Organization, Inc. conducted on behalf o the American Coalition for Entertainment and Sports Sponsorship.

Acceptability of Various Types of Corporate Sponsorship
- Promotional items with corporate I.D.   85%
- Sponsored special events at stadium.   82%
- Corporate logo's or ID on racing cars etc.   82%
- Advertising on food/beverage containers at event.   80%
- Signs in sports stadiums.   78%
- Title sponsorship.   76%
- Corporate logo's or ID on player clothing.   75%
- Distribute corporate brochures at event.   57%

The Importance of Television

A common statement made by sports and event administrators is, *"W don't have television, therefore we cannot attract a sponsor."* They are mistaker In the majority of such cases, the sponsorship required is much smaller thar television coverage would warrant.

Event sponsorship has experienced phenomenal growth over the pas decade. The wealth of marketing options provided by event sponsorship and its ability to deliver highly targeted audiences at a time of increased advertising fragmentation will ensure this growth continues. The vas majority of sponsorships do not have television exposure, yet sponsorship growth continues unabated.

Companies will continue to invest heavily in event sponsorship wher it represents a communication option more effective than conventiona advertising.

"Companies will continue to invest heavily in event sponsorship when it represents a communication option more effective than conventional advertising."

Maximizing Sponsorship Today:

Event marketing is a complex business that requires expertise to achieve optimum results. Inexperience can deny a corporation very extensive exposure and benefits in addition to wasting money. The marketing manager of a potential corporate sponsor needs to be aware of:

- The real cost of sponsorship.
- The benefits of consistency and longevity.
- Marketing disciplines to leverage sponsorship.
- Matching objectives and budget.
- Importance of creativity.
- Event administrators commercial limitations.
- Event sponsorship clutter.
- Managing a corporate sponsorship.
- Ambush marketing.
- Marketing to ethnic groups.

The most important point to be aware of is that the sponsorship is merely a hook on which to build a campaign. It is not a marketing tool in itself. What makes sponsorship work is the disciplines that drive them. In general, if a sponsorship has not paid for itself many times over before the event even takes place, the sponsorship is a failure.

The Real Cost of Sponsorship

In the majority of sponsorships, it is insufficient to merely enter into the sponsorship without a comprehensive supporting campaign.

In most instances sponsorship funds represent only 35-50% of the actual sum needed to maximize the potential benefits of the investment. At least the same amount should support the investment as is spent on the sponsorship itself. Without support marketing and a long term marketing strategy, sponsorship may be ineffectual. Some corporations spend all available funds in the initial sponsorship and have little budget left to make it work for them. Sponsorship packages in most cases will not stand on their own, they need to be part of a total promotional and marketing campaign.

Event sponsorships must be part of an integrated marketing strategy which includes:

1. Advertising. In addition to the event promoter's media spend, the sponsor should advise its target market of its involvement through advertising.
2. Promotion. Promotions to the trade/retailer and/or consumers tied into the sponsorship are an outstanding marketing vehicle. These can stand alone or preferably incorporate other event sponsors to extend reach and cost effectiveness.
3. Public Relations. PR is a very valuable support tool for sponsorships generating substantial third person endorsement to the target audience.
4. On-site Promotion. This includes banners, endorsements, sampling, premium and discount offers, competitions, merchandise and give-aways.

Unless a corporation is prepared to match their sponsorship investment with marketing support, they are wasting their money."

"In general, if a sponsorship has not paid for itself many times over, before the event even takes place, the sponsorship is a failure".

"Sponsorship packages in most cases will not stand on their own, they need to be part of a total promotional and marketing campaign".

5. Off-site Promotion. Promotional tie-ins, sampling, premiums, discounts an displays away from the site greatly increase reach.
6. Hospitality. In an era where shelf space, positioning and trade support imperative, quality relationships with clients are important.
7. Extensions. A host of extensions, from couponing and cause related promotions to celebrity endorsements, all assist in extending the value of th sponsorship.

"Consistency is the key element in achieving high brand recognition."

The additional cost of support is related to the event chosen, the expo sure generated and the sponsor's requirements from the investment. Ever marketing needs to be treated similarly to any other media or marketing con sideration. Before sponsoring any event the corporation should establish:

- The total available budget.
- The sponsorship objectives.
- The additional marketing support necessary to maximize the benefits.
- Their marketing department's ability to handle the project.

Sponsorships Require Consistency and Longevity

Consistency is the key element in achieving high brand recognition Many events have their names changed regularly as sponsors come and g This is not in the best interests of the event or sponsor for the publi become confused, diluting the impact of the sponsor's message.

A major motivation behind sponsorship today is to maximize opportu nities that capture the short term interests of target audiences. There is muc more benefit in long term associations. Such associations create an image corporate commitment, enhance public perception of its good decisions an avoid antagonizing part of the desired market by withdrawing from th sponsorship. By accepting a long term contract, a sponsor can secure bette terms from both the organizers and the media.

In any sponsorship where an integrated marketing strategy employed, a host of unforeseen opportunities will develop. Multi-year spor sorships allow the benefits of these to be maximized in subsequent years.

Matching Sponsor Objectives and Budget

A corporation must decide whether the benefits it seeks from th sponsorship will be affected by co-sponsors. If the corporation is merel seeking hospitality benefits, sharing the sponsorship may result in muc of the cost being offset and the desired results still being achievec Conversely, if the major sponsor is inexperienced in event marketing, can be overshadowed by well-spent support dollars and the skill of bette event marketers.

A growing number of sponsors have in-house event marketin departments or engage event marketing experts and effectively utiliz every available event marketing technique.

Be Creative

With over 5,000 corporations sponsoring teams and events in the United States, it is essential that campaigns be creative in order to stand out and maximize the unique opportunities that event involvement presents.

In 1985, Smartfood Inc., a small undercapitalized company launched a 'healthier' brand of popcorn. With little money for a marketing campaign, they established Smartfood ski, windsurfing and bike teams, a comedy truck and a biplane. The striking black packaging was totally different to anything in the marketplace.

The members of the ski team wore Smartfood costumes and handed out 4,000 to 6,000 samples at a New England ski area each weekend. An old used ice cream truck was remodeled as the 'Yuk Truck' and comics performed from a stage on the roof. The windsurfing teams in Smartfood costumes provided samples to crowds at events. Sales jumped from $35,000 in 1985 to $20 million in 1989.

Corporations need not spend huge amounts to achieve effective results.

"Corporations need not spend huge amounts to achieve effective results."

Smartfood overcame a limited marketing budget by becoming involved in lifestyle activities and sampling the spectators.

Event Administrators Commercial Limitations

An effective sponsorship requires both understanding and co-operation between the sport/event organization, the sponsor and the event marketer. Unless the administrators of the event or the team understand and appreciate the principles of event marketing, the sponsorship is prone to failure.

Reliance on administrators will not work. Often, the only qualification is their former athletic prowess and consequent popularity. Today, an extensive career in advertising, marketing, sales promotion and public relations is the criteria for the role.

When a corporation expects the sponsored event to provide the backup support, it has little chance. Sponsorship must be treated in the same manner as mainstream advertising, utilizing the specialists, developing the extensions and preparing for contingencies.

Managing a Corporate Sponsorship

The event manager should first 'plan' the sponsorship, detailing the various elements, how the benefits can be maximized, the departments or outside agencies required to participate as well as the time and cost involved to properly implement the program. Too many sponsorships have neither the time frame or the budgetary support to drive them effectively.

Throughout the event the object is to maximize results, not have a good time. The attending corporate representatives should be diligent in seeking ways to improve exposure and impact.

From concept to completion, new promotional opportunities continually arise and the event manager must have experience in identifying, negotiating and executing media and retail promotions. If outside agencies are implementing segments of the staging or marketing, the event manager must be aware of every schedule and detail.

In reality, the application of each sponsorship varies depending upon the corporation's objective. The wide variety of event marketing techniques enables each sponsor to reach their target audience and to obtain the benefits sought without their endeavors being negated by another sponsor. The exception occurs when sponsors deliberately go "head to head" or use "ambush marketing" techniques to gain benefit over the opposition.

Ambush Marketing

There is an increasing tendency for corporations who are not official event sponsors to usurp that positioning from the sponsoring corporation. This is achieved by identifying the weakness in the sponsors marketing campaign, nullifying their sponsorship exposure and gain credit for an involvement paid for by their competitor. Protecting the event association is equally the role of sponsor and event because corporations will not pay premiums to support events if their positioning is eroded by a 'non license paying rival. The usual ambush involves heavily advertised promotions that provide an association with the event in the form of merchandise, tickets, billboards, sampling at the event site and association with high profile athlete(s) participating in the event.

Protections against ambush marketing include trade mark and copyright registrations, exclusive control of the event venue rights, including signage, sampling, concessions, effective contracts and clauses which prohibit deals not already in place to be entered into with rival companies until after the event is completed.

Not paying attention to detail also creates situations such as the Toyota ambush at the Chrysler Series Skins Games. Despite an investment of $1 million by Chrysler, the NBC audience clearly identified the Toyota logo on champion Chi Chi Rodriguez shirt.

"Reliance on administrators will not work. Often, the only qualification is their former athletic prowess and consequent popularity."

"Not paying attention to detail enables competitor ambush."

What Can Be Achieved From Sponsorships:

It is necessary to understand the eleven most common sponsorship positioning options available to a corporation before we can maximize the achievement of marketing objectives. Often, it may be a combination of these benefits that is required.These options are;

1. Association with, and access to, the population segment that represents the company's target market.
2. Association with an individual, team or competition that attracts large television or live audiences.
3. Association with success, clean-living, health and fitness.
4. Develop sales opportunities, preferably exclusive.
5. Building relationships with potential future customers.
6. A sponsorship which has prestige, provides prestige.
7. The halo effect, the good citizen image.
8. Association with high profile success.
9. Association with a team or event to tap local or national pride.
10. Association with special interest groups.
11. To develop new markets.

Examples of each of these eleven "benefit" categories:

1.   Association with, and access to, the population segment that represents the company's target market.

This is the most popular motivation for corporate sponsorship investment. Sponsorships such as the "Rank Xerox Marathon" specifically target everyday equipment to the upwardly mobile, decision-making executives who generally represent the majority of participants in these events. The volume of participation guarantees extensive television and other media coverage, either as a televised event, news value, or both. In addition, companies achieve effective grass roots exposure to their target market.

2.   Association with an individual, team or competition that attracts large television or live audiences.

This direct association with success presents the sponsor with the advantage of a large audience. Large television audiences are generally equated to cost efficient advertising, maximum impact from telecast mentions, signage and the loyalty of the supporters of the particular event.

In his book *'Sponsorship'*, Steve Sleight provides the example of Cornhill Insurance Sponsorship of English Test Cricket. In 1977, research showed unprompted awareness of Cornhill was below 2%. Cornhill made a contract with the Test and County Cricket Board (TCCB) for a £1 million sponsorship over 5 years. By November 1977 Cornhills awareness had jumped to 8%, by

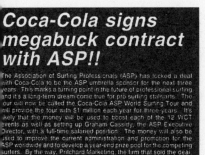

Coca-Cola signs megabuck contract with ASP!!

The Association of Surfing Professionals (ASP) has locked a deal with Coca-Cola to be the ASP umbrella sponsor for the next three years. This marks a turning point in the future of professional surfing, and it's a long-term dream come true for pro surfing stalwarts. The tour will now be called the Coca-Cola ASP World Surfing Tour and will provide the tour with $1 million each year for three years. It's likely that the money will be used to boost each of the 12 WCT events as well as setting up Graham Cassidy, the ASP Executive Director, with a full-time salaried position. The money will also be used to improve the current administration and promotion for the ASP worldwide and to develop a year-end prize pool for the competing surfers. By the way, Pritchard Marketing, the firm that sold the deal, will walk away with a small cut of the dough. Skip Snead

Surfing Magazine
December, 1993

September 1978 it was 13% and in September 1979 it had reached 16%. Interestingly, in the periods between the Test series, the level of awareness fell dramatically, down to as low as 6%, highlighting that sponsorship needs to be constantly reinforced.

Large event attendances enable a sponsor to product sample and promote heavily to a captive audience. Advertising agencies and the majority of corporations often mistakenly believe there is safety in ratings numbers.

3.   Association with Success, Clean Living, Health and Fitness.

When Kellogg sponsored the pro cycling series in Britain, cycling was an emerging sport with a natural tie-in to Corn Flakes. Both are regarded as "healthy for the family." Kellogg promoted the event on 10 million boxes of Bran Flakes, drew 7 hours of TV coverage and tied-in a merchandise offer in over 1,000 outlets. The Kellogg tour, a 6 day cross-country race, became a major event on the European calendar.

The National Potato Board sponsored the U.S. Women's Gymnastics Federation to overcome a public perception of potatoes as fattening. The association with young, fit women is designed to demonstrate that potatoes are important, healthy and good for you.

4.   Develop Sales Opportunities, Preferably Exclusive.

Many local businesses such as insurance companies and car dealerships become involved in sponsorships to obtain access to participants or supporter lists. The company's involvement provides their agents with an emotional hook when following up people on the lists or attracting participants and supporters to the sponsor's outlet.

Brewers and soft drink companies are the principal participants in this sponsorship category because of the opportunities to obtain exclusive pouring rights and sell product at the games, clubs and functions.

The Manna Pro Feed Corporation sponsors the Atlantic Coast Quarter Horse Association. This is an extremely targeted marketing focus on the quarter horse industry expenditure of over a billion dollars annually, much of it on feed.

5.   Building a Relationship With Potential Future Customers.

Banks, insurance companies and radio stations have traditionally sponsored junior sport and coaching clinics in order to develop an awareness and loyalty with youth for a (hopefully) lifetime association.

Avis sponsored the Avis Swimming Championships at UCLA, a team event befitting the Avis theme, "We Try Harder." The discipline of swimming is suggested as a key to successful academic and business careers in a leading academic environment of people who will make the car leasing and rental decisions in corporations of the future.

"Advertising agencies and the majority of corporations often mistakenly believe there is safety in ratings numbers."

6.   A Sponsorship Which has Prestige

Sponsorship of a prestige event can become a flagship for the public perception of the company. The NEC sponsorship of the Davis Cup, the Louis Vitton involvement with the America's Cup, and Visa's sponsorship of the Olympic Games are prime examples.

7.   The Halo Effect.

This is a variation on option six, but rather than positioning the sponsor as a major and prestigious company, it positions the company as "community minded."

American Express has successfully used cause related sponsorships in over 150 programs in 50 markets. This is the linking of a worthwhile cause, for example the Special Olympics, to the corporation through marketing, PR, promotions and special events. The American Express advertising support provides valuable exposure to the cause and encourages substantially increased card usage.

8.   Association with "High Profile Success."

A highly successful team or individual can provide a very positive association for a sponsoring company.

Adidas and Nike are examples of footwear companies who sponsor individual athletes, teams and competitions, suggesting to budding athletes and the public that their peers and idols wear that particular shoe.

9.   Association with a Team to Tap Local or National Pride.

Association with events that invoke the consumer's pride create a very positive response for the sponsor. An *Advertising Age* study showed that 33% of American consumers were more inclined to buy a product if the company was supporting the Olympic Games.

This same principle applies to international competitions. Although sailing has a relatively small following, whole nations enthusiastically support their country's entry in America's Cup events.

The Media Relations Manager for Pepsi, a major sponsor, summed it up. *"Yachting may have limited appeal, but patriotism doesn't."*

10.   Association with Special Interest Groups.

Chevrolet "Geo" capitalized on its position as America's most fuel efficient motor vehicle by sponsoring a number of environmental organizations and planting trees for each vehicle sold. This reinforced in the minds of the substantial ecology conscious market segment that Geo was "the" environment friendly vehicle.

Western Underwriters capitalized on Australia's extraordinary enthusiasm for the America's Cup.

11.   To Develop New Markets.

In the situation where a sport may be very popular but a product may be new, the association of the sponsor with the sport will characterize on the sponsor, increasing awareness and acceptance of the product. This technique also applies to reaching new market segments and geographic areas.

To gain penetration for its new product, Gatorade made its product synonymous with major sports. It appeared as though almost every event on television in the U.S. showed Gatorade coolers, cups and signage at the sidelines. Gatorade provided product, either complimentary or as part of a sponsorship, to some 3,500 events resulting in a retail sales increase from $90 million in 1984 to well over $500 million in 1993.

The Potential Downside:

A sponsorship must reflect well on the sponsor and have absolutely no potential to go awry through adverse media or a bad image of the event or its supporters.

In the aftermath of the Pioneer Paris to Dhakar Rally which left six people dead, Pioneer Electronic Corporation acknowledged that sponsoring the controversial race hurt its image. The Anglo-Dutch firm, DAF BV, said it would never again participate in the rally because it was bad for the company's image.

Selecting the Right Sponsorship:

By allocating each element a numerical value in relation to its importance to the corporation's marketing objectives, Pritchard Marketing has enjoyed considerable success in determining a quantitative comparison of the relative cost-effectiveness of alternate proposals. This approach enables a fast and efficient method of screening proposals to determine those that merit further consideration.

Each of the various influences in the corporation, for example, brand, sales and marketing managers should contribute to the determination of the final formula against which proposed sponsorships are evaluated.

The key to this system is to allocate a value for each element that is important to the corporations marketing strategy. To refine the relative value allotments, apply the determined formula to previous successful and unsuccessful sponsorships and compare the predicted with actual results.

For example, the evaluation criteria and their relative importance may be:

Contribution to brand marketing objectives		10 points
Target market impact		10 points
Sponsorship exclusivity		4 points
Attendance		10 points
Event sales opportunities		5 points
Media exposure	Television	12 points
	Radio	5 points
	Press	4 points
Non-Media exposure		5 points
Hospitality opportunities		15 points
Retailer, wholesaler, distributor involvement		10 points
Quality/position of signage, probable exposure		10 points
Total		**100 Points**

Additional criteria should be added depending on the particular sponsor's objectives.

In this example, if the proposal addresses the target market precisely, 10 points are awarded. If it addresses only half the target market, 5 points are allocated. This process is continued for each benefit.

After completing the procedure for two potential sponsorships, assume alternative A has 80 points while alternative B has 70 points. These figures are then divided by the sponsorship cost providing a relative comparison of the value of each. For example, if both sponsorships are $100,000 asking price, then alternative A's value is 0.8 to B's 0.7.

This procedure provides a number of benefits:

- Enables sponsorship comparison.
- Highlights areas that need to be addressed.
- Provides a comparison of potential and executed performance.
- Allows an on-going assessment of a sponsorship value to the sponsor.

It is absolutely essential in this procedure that the weight given t
each of the elements being evaluated reflects the desired results.

The Check List

Once the event or events that appear to provide the opportunity t
address the corporations marketing objectives are ascertained, the following
check list should be applied as the first step to determine the event to b
sponsored and the benefits sought. By carefully evaluating each item, th
marketing support required in terms of advertising, collateral, manpowe
and funds can also be determined.

Primary Check List

1. What are the objectives of the sponsorship?
2. Are the target audiences of the event and sponsor compatible?
3. Is it geographically compatible?
4. What is the event history, performance, public perception?
5. Does the sponsorship cost fit the budget?
6. Does the activity have sufficient reach?
7. Does it fit the sponsor's selling period?
8. Is a previous sponsor already identified with the event?
9. Is another sponsor identified generically with the particular sport/activity
10. How many other sponsors are there? Is there clutter, compatibility?
11. Does it reach a particularly critical segment of your market?
12. Is the activity compatible with the marketing strategy?
13. Do your competitors sponsor similar activities?
14. Is the event a one-time event or does it provide an ongoing program?
    Is this important?
15. Are there legal or insurance difficulties?

Once the answers to these questions are evaluated, the next phase
is to determine the exact requirements sought by the sponsorship.

Secondary Check List

1. Is event attendance important?
2. Is event signage important? If so, is it the amount, the overall percentag
   or the positioning that is important?
3. Is media important? Identify whether local, regional or national,
   broadcast or print.
4. How much advertising is the event promoter doing? How much of
   this will identify the sponsor?
5. Will retailers, wholesalers or distributors support the program?
6. Will they buy additional stock, display product and point of sale material
7. Does the trade need to be tied in?
8. Does the event provide incentive or opportunity for the sales team,
   employees?
9. Can the event be assimilated with the current advertising, sales promo
   tion or publicity campaign?

10. Can a sales promotion or advertising campaign be built around the event?
11. Is hospitality important? Are there sufficient hospitality opportunities available, pre-event and at the activity, for VIP and others?
12. Are there exclusive sales opportunities at the event?
13. Are there merchandise benefits, either at the event or through licensing?
14. Are sampling opportunities available?
15. Is a charity tie-in important?
16. Can celebrities be tied in to the sponsorship?

These points will determine the basic platform from which to negotiate with the event promoter to shape the final sponsorship package. From the potential sponsor's viewpoint, there are still a number of aspects that need to be addressed and this is the third phase.

Tertiary Check List

1. Can the event be extended into additional events or markets?
2. Are there opportunities to develop secondary events to support the main activity?
3. Is in-house expertise available to manage the sponsorship?
4. Is the sponsorship cost-effective?

It is essential to reiterate that every sponsorship must be tailor-made to suit a particular corporation's goals. For example, in the case of a consumer product, the sponsor should seek to obtain exposure at the point of purchase; case and off-shelf displays, counter card and mobiles, sales and trade incentives, and tie-ins with product packages to assist impulse buying.

The sponsor should be prepared to tag media advertising for the event in the same way the event does for the sponsor.

In order to impact on those who do not attend the event, the organizer and the sponsor should work together to maximize off-site visibility with promotions at high traffic locations, sampling, schedule cards, bumper stickers and so on.

Corporate sponsors need to realize that event sponsorship on its own will not usually create the urge to buy a product. But neither will advertising. Event sponsorships support lifestyle characterization of the product or service and a well targeted sponsorship will cause supporters to relate to the product. Consistent favorable impressions will lead to sales.

Check out the event organizers. Reaching agreement with an event for a sponsorship does not guarantee that benefits promised will be delivered. Before signing the contract, the sponsor should complete due diligence on the organizer. This should include evaluating their experience, performance, whether any legal difficulties exist, and insurance liability. Previous sponsor references should be obtained.

Making the Sponsorship Work:

Sponsorships in many ways are like advertising campaigns. Many campaigns have won Clio Awards but did not increase sales. In fact, some advertising campaigns have actually decreased sales.

Sponsorships all offer "benefits," the critical question is whether they are actually of benefit to the potential corporate sponsor. Ten million impacts on national television are probably useless if the company's distribution is only in Southern California.

The problem is not locating a sponsorship, there are literally thousands available. The difficulty in selecting a sponsorship is ensuring it is compatible with the corporation's overall marketing strategy, can achieve the desired objectives and provide marketing extensions geared to specific goals at a cost comparable to available alternatives.

Different sponsors require different benefits. For example, what is the value to Coca-Cola or Pepsi of a sign at an event? Their level of public awareness is almost 100%. They require a sponsorship that provides opportunities to obtain pouring rights or to assist distributors to move product off shelves. Each sponsorship must be custom made to satisfy the objectives of the particular corporation.

The following general points are worth remembering:

1. Large crowds and television viewing audiences do not necessarily mean a successful sponsorship. An event success does not necessarily guarantee the sponsor's message was heard.

2. Sponsored events need not necessarily be televised to achieve their objectives. Excellent sponsorships are available with relatively small non-televised exposure and small attendances. If the marketing objective is right, the exposure, collateral material and public relations benefits may provide outstanding low-cost opportunities. Exposure value to cost ratio is the important factor.

3. Event administrators often over-inflate the value of a sponsorship or have little idea of its worth. A sponsor needs to determine its objectives and negotiate the sponsorship conditions that meet its requirements rather than buying the package offered.

4. Event organizers respect money. The greater the sum, the greater the respect. Support sponsors need to constantly liaise with organizers and work a lot harder to obtain the event organizer's respect and assistance in making the sponsorship work than does the title sponsor.

5. For many sponsors not requiring strong consumer brand imaging, secondary sponsorships can be more cost-effective and allow for a more targeted pitch than the title. For example, it may be advantageous to spend the savings between the cost of the title and the support on hospitality for distributors of the corporation's product.

6. Ensure the event is supported by advertising, not just publicity. Publicity is speculative, not controllable, guaranteed or predictable. This also applies to nearly all of the other communication techniques that extend the promotion.

"Event organizers respect money. The greater the sum, the greater the respect."

7.   Television tries to minimize sponsor exposure, so use drink cups, towels, sun visors and other items to obtain coverage.

Sponsorship Planning

There are a number of rules to follow when planning sponsorships.

Establish objectives

Clearly articulate the specific objectives to be sought from the sponsorship. These may include brand awareness to a particular target market, on-site concessions, developing trade relationships, product endorsement, national or international exposure and so on.

Match the sponsorship with the target market

It is necessary to understand the demographic and psychographic (mind set) characteristics of the target market, their attitudes and their interests. Knowledge of relative event popularity and the supporters usage of the sponsors product or affinity to the product is important.

Ensure event and product synergy

Many events have definite images that may either enhance or have a negative effect on the companies product image.

Relate to the event supporters

The benefits of the sponsorship must be designed to have a maximum favorable impact on the event follower. It is essential to determine how this can be achieved.

Define the catchment areas

Research can identify geographic regions where there are high concentrations of target market users, often an essential criteria in event selection. This enables cost effective marketing through specific retail outlets, promotions, direct mail, assistance in defining stock levels of merchandise and locations for promotional activity.

Ascertain media habits

It is essential to understand the media preference of the target market audience to ensure the most cost effective communication.

Select the appropriate level of involvement

This depends entirely on the sponsorship objectives. If the objective is to provide hospitality and this option is not available on its own, then often the least expensive involvement providing this opportunity will be effective. If seeking brand awareness, a logo on a tennis ball travelling at 110 miles per hour is ineffective to say the least.

Longevity

In the majority of instances, the benefits of sponsorship increase wi**
time. A greater understanding of the event, increased involvement by di
tributors and retailers enable expansion of extension opportunities.

The Sponsorship is just the Beginning

Entering into a sponsorship agreement with an event will not, on i
own, achieve the marketing objectives. This step merely provides the co
poration with a hook on which to develop an effective marketing campaig

Retail Leveraging

To increase retailer support, gain more in-store presence and incl**
sion in the various retailer advertising and promotions mediums, sponso
need to create retailer and consumer incentives. This can be achieved b
purchase incentives, an incremental promotional spend, event ticket
media cross-promotions to drive traffic, exclusive hospitality or rights to
traffic building in-store promotion. To maximize retail involvement, it
preferable to create specific promotional hooks, customized to each retai
er, in lieu of a non-specific market wide promotion.

Often a sponsor will provide the retailer with their event benefits i
exchange for end-of-aisle displays, a prime location or a specific case orde

Traffic Builders

Appearances by athletes or performers, a race car replica or a nov
participatory activity such as virtual reality, flight or race car simulato
build store traffic.

A common promotion by motor racing sponsors is to offer pit passe
V.I.P. tickets, merchandise and invitations to exclusive "team only" activ
ties in return for a specific order, extra shelf space, end-of-aisle display
and advertising pull through in other retailer exposure medium
Additional "incentives" can be provided for consumers on a purchase (
proof-of-purchase basis.

Driving Sales

Consumers are incentivated to buy by techniques such as on-pack, i
pack, sweepstakes, rebates, discount event tickets or merchandise. Thes
offers are driven by in-store displays, product tag or on-label promotio
p.o.p. and advertising. Sales can also be generated by the sponsors contr
bution to a particular charity or activity based on product sales.

Adding value to a purchase by offering a limited purchase opportu
nity, preferential seating or an exclusive involvement will encourage buy
ers. On-pack or in-pack collectables or premiums provide sponsors wit
an opportunity to self liquidate their investment.

> "If seeking brand
> awareness, a logo on
> a tennis ball travelling
> at 110 miles per hour is
> ineffective to say the least."

Maximizing the Opportunities

Sponsorship promotions should be structured to involve not only the consumer, but also distributors, retailers and the media. The consumer can be offered tickets, event video's or merchandise, the distributors obtain exclusive hospitality opportunities, the retailers can receive event signage, television billboards and shared sponsorship rights with the media receiving event exposure or an exclusive high energy promotion.

"Sponsorship can carve out a niche and differentiate cosponsors from one another."

Co-sponsor cross promotions can also greatly enhance the reach and impact of a sponsorship or penetrate new markets without increasing the sponsorship support investment.

To create co-sponsor involvement, discussions by the various parties on their marketing objectives, media and retail support, potential areas of increasing exposure by inclusion in other sponsors campaigns, areas of cost savings such as advertising production, photography, graphics and so on need to be held. Mutual promotions can be staged with shared cost.

Sweepstakes, offering prizes from the various co-sponsors can increase their effectiveness and appeal, while reducing costs.

Sponsoring events can also open the doors for sponsors to develop a relationship with venue concessionaires and get their product sold not only during the event but on an ongoing basis.

Recruiting Media Partners

Media outlets are constantly seeking event tie-ins that will appeal to their target audience, enhance the value of their advertising and differentiate themselves from their competitors. Often event tie-ins provide the opportunity for event promotions or on-site outside broadcasts. These activities enhance their audience relationship. For an event organizer, the relationship the media outlet sales forces enjoy with the corporate sector can provide an excellent source of event sponsorship. The media outlet will frequently provide an accompanying promotion adding significantly to both the event and sponsors exposure.

"Unless corporations can obtain a better return on their investment through sponsorships than through normal media, the current sponsorship boom will fade."

It is these types of promotional ties and add-on incentives that enable sponsors to carve out a niche and differentiate themselves from both co-sponsor's and competitors.

Conclusion

Too many corporations have assumed the sponsorship will work for itself, committing little or no expertise to its implementation. For event sponsorship to achieve the exceptional benefits of which it is capable, it must be extended into sales promotion, merchandising, direct marketing, public relations and the other marketing tools that are available.Unless corporations can obtain a better return on their investment through sponsorships than through normal media, the current sponsorship boom will fade.

Case Studies

1. **Members Only** sought greater awareness for its sports apparel lines. PM provided then ranked heavyweight Evander Holyfield with Members Only trunks and robe, track suits and caps for the trainers and entourage prior to the World Championship bout with Buster Douglas. In addition to providing the clothing, a fee was paid to Holyfield. In return, Members Only received prime television and event exposure, excellent ring side tickets for management and contest winners and prime exposure at pre and post-event media conferences.

The Result? Evander won the world title and Members Only received world media exposure. Careful event targeting produced worldwide front page exposure for the sponsor.

2. **General Mills** sought to introduce its Granola Bars to an upmarket healthy lifestyle consumer. PMI secured sponsorship of the World Cup of Freestyle Skiing at Breckenridge, Colorado for the company.

In addition to prime television signage, hospitality for clients/consumers and billboard television exposure, a Granola Bar was sampled to every person buying a lift ticket at any of 15 booths during event week.

Integral to comprehensive planning, a trial sampling revealed a potential littering problem. PMI proactively positioned "General Mills Cares for the Environment" waste bins across the slopes, enhancing the company's exposure and adding an important ecological facet to its sponsorship.

During event week, the unrelated Ulr Festival was being held in Breckenridge. PMI was able to secure banners in the parade as well as radio and public address exposure for General Mills to the huge festival audience at no cost to the client.

3. **Nissay Insurance of Japan**, one of the world's largest insurance companies asked PMI to create a major event as an incentive for their sales staff. PMI created a client customized ice skating production which featured Olympic Gold Medalists Katarina Witt, Robin Cousins and sixteen other Olympians. We shipped a stadium size ice rink from Los Angeles to Japan as no large size skating venues existed in that country.

Creativity, initiative and attention to detail produced a unique and powerful motivation program for 35,000 Nissay employees and their families halfway around the world.

4. **The Coca-Cola Company's** title sponsorship of the globally televised A.S.P. 65 event, 6 continent, $30 million World Championship Tour was only the third global sponsorship in the company's 107 year history, the other two being the Olympic Games and World Cup Soccer.

PMI supervises every aspect of Coca-Cola's involvement including television, event signage, advertising, promotion, collateral, hospitality and liaising with regional Coke management and bottlers.

5. **Maxicare Health Systems** sought increased identification with the senior market. PMI secured the title sponsorship of "Time of Your Life," the world's largest expos for people 50 and older. TOYL produced literally millions of collateral pieces, advertised extensively in all senior's and leisure magazines, local and metropolitan newspapers, on television and radio. Maxicare received prime positioning in all of this exposure, extensive event signage, live presentations several times each day from center stage and prime booth space throughout the expo.Perfect demographic targeting produced over 150 million impacts on their target market, communicated their message to large groups of their target audience and the ability to interface with them, one-on-one.

6. **American Express'** objective was to obtain increased card acceptance from vendors while concurrently employing the increased acceptance as a marketing and promotional vehicle. PMI obtained "Preferred Credit Card" status for the company with Theater L.A., the 108 member association of Los Angeles theaters. The American Express card was immediately accepted at all Theater L.A. locations and venues where previously few of the theaters accepted the card.

In addition to obtaining access to 2.8 million ticket buyers, American Express received signage and promotions in all theaters, exposure in advertising and promotion, hundreds of free tickets and exceptional theater and restaurant cross promotion opportunities. Theater LA pro-moted the company in all its membership mail-outs, at receptions and other events, including the prestigious Ovation Awards.

7. **Kenwood Electronics** required a sponsorship vehicle for its audio division that would impact a young, upwardly mobile, fun loving consumer. PMI proposed the title sponsorship of a series of beach volleyball events at beaches located close to their dealerships.

There was one catch... it was important to include Phoenix, Arizona in the program. To address this, PMI built a beach in the parking lot of the Pointe Resort, the first time it had ever been done. The result was an overwhelming success. In addition to a national television broadcast of each event, live radio tie-ins, naming rights exposure in all advertising, promotion and collateral, in-store promotions, on-beach audio promotions and great hospitality, all the events attracted huge crowds. The biggest attendance? Phoenix, where the client's target market consumers, dressed in beach attire, turned the event into a promotional bonanza for Kenwood.

8. **Pavilions Grocery Stores** sought an involvement that reinforced its positioning as a premier grocery retailer. PMI obtained the sponsorship of the opening night of the world renowned Los Angeles Philharmonic Orchestra for the company. This prestigious sponsorship provided Pavilions with extensive exposure through advertising, promotion and the city wide newspaper inserts and direct mail campaign carried out by the Philharmonic. The involvement attracted customers to their stores to purchase tickets, created a perfect sales vehicle for Pavilions' picnic baskets and enabled it to retail flowers at the Hollywood Bowl.

PMI created an end-of-aisle promotional display in all Pavilions stores tying in brands that could be associated with the "picnic hamper program." The result; the financial contribution from the brands liquidated the cost of Pavilions sponsorship.

Centerfold

FROM THE FRONT: THE SELLING OF A GLOBAL SPONSORSHIP The Coca-Cola Co's. first-time, three-year multimillion-dollar sponsorship of the Assn. of Surfing Professionals resulted from nearly two years of research and negotiation by Pritchard Marketing. Below, the agency's chairman, Bob Pritchard, describes how the deal developed.

In September 1991, ASP appointed Pritchard as its exclusive agency with a charge to review global operations and recommend ways to enhance the viability of its World Championship Tour and World Qualifying Tour, which now have a total of 67 stops in 23 countries. At the time, the sanctioning body had negligible information on audience demographics, attendance, media exposure or even which TV stations broadcast its events.

We spent the next three months gathering that data, as well as details on event advertising, collateral material, press coverage and opportunities for on-site signage, hospitality, sales and promotions We contacted event organizers, ASP's five regional directors and magazines and TV stations across five continents to determine how much exposure the tour received.

In March '92, we recommended to Graham Cassidy ASP executive director, that ASP solicit a global umbrella sponsor; form a separate, for-profit marketing arm and create a major event on the U.S. mainland. No such event had existed since ASP established its two tier structure of WCT and WQT events in 1990. We also wanted to increase prize money and medical coverage and services for competitors, as well as raise ASP's profile by placing inserts and wraparounds in major surfing magazines and by establishing a media unit in each tour market and international newsstand distribution of the Tour Guide.

We determined that accomplishing those objectives would require a first-year sponsorship fee of $1.2 million. A second-year fee of $1.58 million would go toward adding electronic scoreboards, investing in ASP's women's tour and creating Legends of Surfing and wave-pool circuits. The final year's fee of $1.75 million would add coaching clinics in each tour region. ASP could justify the fees in part by integrating the sponsor's name into its logo and offering joint ownership of the new mark.

Cassidy approved the package in April. We then submitted ou research, along with the framework of benefits ASP could offer global sponsor, to the regional directors. When we mentione plans to target Coke, the directors voiced concern about losing on site beverage sales rights, a significant source of revenue, so w agreed that events would retain those rights as long as they did no sell product in competition with Coke.

(What Coke regards as competition-all carbonated and non carbonated beverages, fruit juices, sports beverages, bottle waters and milk-based drinks-affects several ASP event sponsor around the world, a situation we and the local Coke bottlers ar negotiating to resolve.

For example, Yoplait, which titles the Reunion Island Worl Championship Tour stop, has agreed to promote only its yogur and not its milk drinks. Another event with a milk sponsor mus break off that relationship if the stop is to remain sanctioned Coke is trying to persuade its bottler in the region to cover th event's resulting loss of revenue.

Also, to appease regional directors we modified signage t accommodate local event sponsors. After all ASP parties wer satisfied with what we would offer a sponsor. we entered discus sions with various TV placement organizations and networks such as Brazil's TV Globo and Belgium's Sports Vision, to deter mine the potential increase in programming they would carry.

Although we made no sponsor ad commitment, each grou agreed to more consistent delivery and solicitation of new mar kets for programming on their respective continents. Since 1990 those networks and others throughout the world-including ESPN Prime Network and MTV-have telecast programs produced fo ASP by San Clemente, Calif.-based DynoComm Productions.

Agency To Agency. In July. we initiated discussions wit Mark Buckman, senior vice president of international media. an Tor Sirset, international media supervisor, both at Coke's a agency, New York City-based McCann-Erickson. We alway customize proposals for potential sponsors, but it often is difficu to get the feedback necessary to do this from a swamped corpo rate marketing director.

That is why we regularly approach a potential sponsor' agency first. By enlisting the support of an agency with a com plete understanding of its client's long-term strategic plan, we ca develop a package specific to those criteria. In addition, agenc personnel often have a relationship with client decision maker that ensures the proposal will receive proper evaluation.

McCann objected to the proposal's lack of a U.S. mainland event, which ASP had yet to establish. Within weeks, ASP agreed to underwrite the $400,000 to $500,000 cost of creating such an event and asked us to begin soliciting sponsors. McCann also asked us to devise promotions that Coke could use to extend its investment.

Before seeing our full proposal the agency told us surfing was last on a 100-sport list at Coke headquarters. To counter that, we provided details and results of a six-week promotion around Coke Australia's title sponsorship of a local ASP stop, including incremental sales of more than 80 million "Coke Classic Surf" branded cans. We also submitted competition details. posters, collateral materials, licensed merchandise and premiums and copies of radio and TV ads. Still, McCann said Coke would require "beefed up" TV exposure, that long-distance shots of surfers riding waves did not benefit the sponsor.

Throughout September, we worked with McCann to tailor TV distribution and exposure in various parts of the world and to gather more and better demographic information. We also worked with *Surfer Magazine's* circulation, ad sales and overseas distributors to solicit data on the sport's popularity and exposure in the 77 countries the publication reaches.

In addition. we examined televised surfing programs and scripted a format that increased the number of exposures for Coke signage, drink cups, hats, towels and other items and enhanced viewer interest and involvement.

In October, we and McCann developed the final sponsorship package in two proposals: one delineated the benefits to Coke corporately, the other detailed benefits and opportunities, such as hospitality and surfer appear- ances, available to each bottler in event regions.

We began preparing our presentation for Chuck Fruit, vice president, director of global advertising and media, and Gary Hite, vice president, international sports consulting and planning, at Coke headquarters. We delivered the presentation in January '93 nearly six months after first approaching McCann. During that time we solicited no other sponsors.

(We always work on a fee to cover our costs and then receive a commission from our client when the program comes to fruition. Part of Coke's ASP sponsorship fee offsets the costs we incur managing the tie, which entails a staffer traveling with the tour to meet local bottlers and help implement programs.)

In late January, McCann advised us that Coke required more ad time to make the sponsorship worth the investment so we re-contacted the media distributors and networks, seeking the addition of a free 30 second commercial within each hour of coverage. We received approval for spots in 160 hours of programming, about 60 percent of all broadcasts.

We also negotiated more ways to increase sponsor exposure within the programs, taking into account various regulations from country to country. For example, broadcasters in some countries do not allow billboards or bumpers and limit the number of drop-ins. Consequently, we will produce three different versions of the same program, perhaps interviewing a competitor standing in front of a Coke logo in one version and without the logo in another.

Meanwhile, we and ASP accelerated development of a format for stadium surfing. The 38 "indoor beach" venues around the world, which produce regulated waves every 12 seconds, enable the staging of events with a music and light show for a paying audience. We combined a six stop pool series to launch in '95 with the existing package to give Coke more exposure and other opportunities.

In February, McCann presented the revised package to Coke. The company and agency disseminated it to the respective offices around the world for feedback because funding would come from participating Coke regions. In March, McCann advised us that financial constraints due to Coke's new global ad campaign and uncertainty by a couple of the regions made the sponsorship unlikely.

Pitching The Competition. We immediately contacted Brian Swette senior vice president, new beverage business at Pepsi-Cola Co. headquarters; Bill Waters media manager at Pepsi Cola West; Don Skeoch marketing manager at Pepsi-Cola Southern Callifornia and Peter Scott, sponsorship director at Lion Nathan Breweries, which owns the Pepsi license for Australia and New Zealand in addition to accounting for about half the beer market there.

We sent each of them a proposal with an increased emphasis on the new California WCT event which would be presented in '94 by Prime Ticket TV network. We then met with Scott to customize the proposal even further for Pepsi which wanted more of a cutting-edge, MTV look and more focus on licensed merchandise to leverage at retail.

Since a Coke sponsorship seemed unlikely, we granted Pepsi a three-month window during which we would sign no other sponsors. Meanwhile, McCann kept in touch with us on our progress with Pepsi. As Pepsi's exclusive deadline drew near, Coke approached us to renew discussions after gaining the necessary support from region bottlers.

On July 22, Coke asked us to send an updated sponsorship proposal, now 67 pages long, to lan Rowden, director of Coca-Cola South Pacific, at the Coke marketing meeting in Singapore. We advised Rowden that we needed a decision before Sept. 6. That was the day we were presenting the board with detailed plans for the ASP's restructure and establishment of ASP Properties. Funding of these changes required us to have a global sponsor in place.

On Sept. 3, we received Rowden's fax accepting the sponsorship. Constant swapping of Coke and Pepsi in the Pritchard boardroom refrigerator-depending on the visitor was over.

Pritchard Marketing *Tel: U.S. 310-451-4748. Aust: 02-9957-2927.*

BOB PRITCHARD

Few people have enjoyed a marketing career with the success and diversity that Bob Pritchard has over the past 20 years. As Marketing Manager for Kerry Packer's PBL Marketing he rose to prominence as Australia's highest profile and successful marketing entrepreneur. The seven nation World Series Cricket "revolution", the Kiri Te Kanawa tour and his role in the inaugural Australian Formula 1 Grand Prix (which, on its debut, won international acclaim as the best Grand Prix of the Year) established his credibility.

The controversial and outspoken marketer conceived and engineered the first private ownership of a major sports team in Australia, the Sydney professional AFL football team and as Chief Executive increased the team's attendance by over 350% in one season. His role as Marketing Director for the internationally televised Norman, Watson, Nicklaus, Ballesteros Skin's game and the America's Cup launch in Sydney further enhanced his reputation.

Since moving to America in the mid eighties, Pritchard's career has mushroomed. He created and implemented one of only three international marketing programs involving sport in Coca-Cola's Atlanta's 107 year history and is responsible for its on going implementation. Evander Holyfield, Katarina Witt, the Los Angeles Philharmonic, the Boy's Choir of Harlem, the World Cup of Freestyle Skiing are just a few of the properties who have benefited from the Pritchard expertise.

Planning, negotiating and managing international tours for a host of properties and working with corporations such as General Motors, Ford, Coca-Cola and American Express and his position on the board of the 285 station Sports Radio Network and 115 station business News Network adds to his vast experience. The Pritchard organization also created the high tech automated event ticket and merchandise kiosks being installed in high traffic outlets across the United States.

Despite travelling extensively for corporate clients, Pritchard has written an event marketing textbook described as the most comprehensive ever written on the subject and the acclaimed "Complex Marketing Made Simple". He is in constant demand as a speaker, his hallmarks being his entertaining and dynamic delivery, meticulous preparation and practical take away value. Bob Pritchard has been recognized for his achievements in many ways including being featured on "60 Minutes" and being the first Australian to be included in the Who's Who in American Advertising.

Craig Johnson and The F.A. Cup.

Nigel Mansell, Formula 1 World Champion.

Kenny Rogers on Tour.